Books are to be returned on or before
the last date below.

2 4 SEP 2004

2 8 APR 2006

LIBREX —

Second Language Acquisition Research
Theoretical and Methodological Issues

Susan Gass and Jacquelyn Schachter, Editors

Tarone/Gass/Cohen • Research Methodology in Second Language Acquisition

Schachter/Gass • Second Language Classroom research: Issues and Opportunities

Birdsong • Second Language Acquisition and the Critical Period Hypothesis

Ohta • Second Language Acquisition Processes in the Classroom: Learning Japanese

Major • Foreign Accent: Ontogeny and Phylogeny of Second Language Phonology

---

Monographs on Research Methodology

Gass/Mackey • Stimulated Recall Methodology in Second Language Research

Yule • Referential Communication Tasks

Markee • Conversation Analysis

Dörnyei • Questionnaires in Second Language Research: Construction, Administration, and Processing

---

Of Related Interest

Gass/Sorace/Selinker • Second Language Learning Data Analysis, Second Edition

Gass/Selinker • Second Language Acquisition: An Introductory Course, Second Edition

Questionnaires in Second Language Research

Construction, Administration, and Processing

Zoltán Dörnyei

University of Nottingham

LEA LAWRENCE ERLBAUM ASSOCIATES, PUBLISHERS

2003 Mahwah, New Jersey London

The camera ready copy for the text of this book was provided by the author.

Lawrence Erlbaum Associates, Inc., Publishers
10 Industrial Avenue
Mahwah, New Jersey 07430

Cover design by Kathryn Houghtaling Lacey

Library of Congress Cataloging-in-Publication Data

Dörnyei, Zoltán.
   Questionnaires in second language research : construction, administration,
and processing / Zoltán Dörnyei.
      p.   cm.
   Includes bibliographical references and index.
   ISBN 0-8058-3908-9 (acid-free paper) – ISBN 0-8058-3909-7 (acid-
   free paper)
      1. Second language acquisition–Research–Methodology.
   2. Questionnaires. I. Title.

P118.2 .D67 2002
418'.007'2–dc21

                                                                2002071290

Printed in the United States of America
10 9 8 7 6 5 4 3 2

Contents

Introduction

One of the most common methods of data collection in second language (L2) research is to use *questionnaires* of various kinds. The popularity of questionnaires is due to the fact that they are easy to construct, extremely versatile, and uniquely capable of gathering a large amount of information quickly in a form that is readily processable. Indeed, the frequency of use of self-completed questionnaires as a research tool in the L2 field is surpassed only by that of language proficiency tests.

In spite of the wide application of questionnaires in the L2 field, there does not seem to be sufficient awareness in the profession about the theory of questionnaire design and processing. The usual – and in most cases false – perception is that anybody with a bit of common sense can construct a good questionnaire. This situation resembles somewhat the 'pre-scientific' phase of language testing (i.e., the period before the 1950s) when language tests were used without paying enough attention to their psychometric qualities, and every language teacher was, by definition, assumed to be capable of devising and grading tests and exams without any special training. It is my impression that many questionnaire users are unaware of the fact that there is considerable relevant knowledge and experience accumulated in various branches of the social sciences (e.g., psychometrics, social psychology, sociology). This is why it is all too common to find studies which start out with exciting research questions but are flawed by a badly designed or inadequately processed questionnaire.

In one sentence...

"The essential point is that good research cannot be built on poorly collected data..."

(Gillham, 2000, p. 1)

This book is intended to be practical in nature. During the past 15 years I have found questionnaire theory to be very helpful in my own research. I designed my first questionnaire in the mid-1980s for my PhD work and because my specialization area – the study of L2 motivation – is very closely linked to the use of questionnaires, I have since then taken part as a principal researcher, participant, or supervisor in numerous studies surveying over 10,000 learners. The idea to share my experience in the use of questionnaires with a broader audience occurred to me last year when I was working on the research section of a book on motivation (Dörnyei, 2001), and thanks to the encouragement I have received from Susan Gass right from the beginning, the initial idea has eventually lead to this book.

Although questionnaire design, and more generally, survey research, has a substantial literature in the social sciences, this has not been sufficiently reflected in L2 methodology texts. With the emphasis typically placed on research methods and statistical procedures in them, there was simply not enough room for discussing specific research instruments (with the sole exception of language tests), and the issue of 'questionnaires' has usually been summarized in a maximum of 3-4 pages. It was therefore a real surprise that, while already working on this book, I learned about another book in the making on a related topic: J. D. Brown's (2001) *"Using Surveys in Language Programs."* As it happened, the two books are largely complementary, with few overlaps. I was fortunate to have JD's manuscript in my hands when preparing the final draft of this book (thanks once again, JD!) and I will refer you to it at times for a more detailed discussion of certain topics.

The structure of the book is straightforward. After an initial chapter that discusses the nature, the merits, and the shortcomings of questionnaires, separate chapters cover the construction and the administration of the questionnaire, as well as the processing of questionnaire data. The book is concluded by a detailed checklist that summarizes the main principles and recommendations.

1

Questionnaires in Second Language Research

Asking questions is one of the most natural ways of gathering information and, indeed, as soon as babies have mastered the basics of their mother tongue they launch into a continuous flow of questions, and keep going throughout the rest of their lives. Some people such as reporters actually make a living of this activity and survey/polling organizations can base highly successful businesses on it.

Because the essence of *scientific research* is trying to find answers to questions in a systematic manner, it is no wonder that the *questionnaire* has become one of the most popular research instruments applied in the social sciences. Questionnaires are certainly *the* most often employed data collection devices in statistical work, with the most well-known questionnaire type – the *census* – being the flagship of every national statistical office.

The main strength of questionnaires is the ease of their construction. In an age of computers and sophisticated word processing software it is possible to draw up something that looks respectable in a few hours. After all, as Gillham (2000) reminds us, we all know what questionnaires look like: hardly a week goes by without some coming our way. Ironically, the strength of questionnaires is at the same time also their main weakness. People appear to take it for granted that everybody with reasonable intelligence can put together a questionnaire that works. Unfortunately, this is not true: Just like in everyday life where not every question elicits the right answer, it is all too common in scientific investigations to come across questionnaires that fail. In fact, I believe that *most* questionnaires applied in second language (L2) research are somewhat *ad hoc* instruments, and questionnaires with sufficient (and well-documented) psychometric reliability and validity are not that easy to come by in our field. This is of course no accident: In spite of the growing methodological awareness that has characterized applied linguistics over the past two decades, the practice of questionnaire design/use has remained largely uninformed by theory. I sometimes wonder what proportion of questionnaire constructors are actually aware that such a theory exists...

Not indeed...

"The world is full of well-meaning people who believe that everyone who can write plain English and has a modicum of common sense can produce a good questionnaire. This book is not for them."

(Oppenheim, 1992, p. 1)

As already mentioned in the Introduction, my interest in questionnaires is pragmatic and practice-driven. I use them all the time and I would like the measures obtained by them to meet high research standards. Having fallen into many of the existing pitfalls several times, I intend for this book to offer concrete suggestions on how to use questionnaires to best effect and how to save ourselves a lot of trouble. Drawing on my own experience and a review of the literature, I will summarize the main principles of constructing and administering questionnaires, and outline the key issues in processing and reporting questionnaire data.

I would like to emphasize right at the onset that this is a 'questionnaire book,' which means that I will not go into much detail about issues that go beyond the immediate scope of the subject; for example, I will not elaborate on topics such as overall survey design, statistical procedures, or qualitative data analysis. There are many good summaries that cover these issues well, and I have listed some that I have found particularly useful in the past in the 'Further reading' section on page 5.

Further reading

There is no shortage of books on questionnaires; many relevant and useful works have been written on the topic in such diverse disciplines as psychology, measurement theory, statistics, sociology, educational studies, and market research. In the L2 field a very recent volume by J. D. Brown (2001) provides a comprehensive account of survey research (which uses questionnaires as one of the main data gathering instruments), offering a detailed account of how to process questionnaire data either statistically or qualitatively. In the field of psychological measurement, two companion volumes by Aiken (1996, 1997) provide up-to-date overviews of questionnaires, inventories, rating scales, and checklists. Of the many books specifically focusing on questionnaire design I would like to highlight three: Oppenheim's (1992) summary is the revised version of his classic work from 1966, and Sudman and Bradburn's (1983) monograph is also a seminal volume in the area. Finally, Gillham's (2000) recent slim monograph is refreshing with its readable and entertaining style.

1.1 WHAT ARE 'QUESTIONNAIRES' AND WHAT DO THEY MEASURE?

Although the term 'questionnaire' is one that most of us are familiar with, it is not a straightforward task to provide a precise definition for it. To start with, the term is partly a misnomer because many questionnaires do *not* contain any, or many, real questions that end with a question mark. Indeed, questionnaires are often referred to under different names, such as 'inventories,' 'forms,' 'opinnionaires,' 'tests,' 'batteries,' 'checklists,' 'scales,' 'surveys,' 'schedules,' 'studies,' 'profiles,' 'indexes/indicators,' or even simply 'sheets' (Aiken, 1997).

Second, the general rubric of 'questionnaire' has been used by researchers in at least two broad senses:

(a) *Interview schedules*, like the ones used in opinion polls, when someone actually conducts a live interview with the respondent, reading out a set of fixed questions and marking the respondent's answers on an answer sheet.

(b) *Self-administered pencil-and-paper questionnaires*, like the 'consumer surveys' that we often find in our mail box or the short forms we are asked to fill in when, for example, checking out of a hotel to evaluate the services.

In this book – in accordance with Brown's (2001) definition below – I will concentrate on the second type only, that is, on the self-completed, written questionnaire that respondents fill in by themselves. More specifically, the focus will be on questionnaires employed as research instruments for measurement purposes to collect reliable and valid data.

A definition for 'questionnaires'

"Questionnaires are any written instruments that present respondents with a series of questions or statements to which they are to react either by writing out their answers or selecting from among existing answers."

(Brown, 2001, p. 6)

1.1.1 What a questionnaire is not

Tests are not questionnaires

Written, self-completed (or self-report) questionnaires are very similar to written tests, yet there is a basic difference between them. A 'test' takes a sample of the respondent's behavior/knowledge and, on the basis of this sample, inferences are made about the degree of the development of the individual's more general underlying competence/abilities/skills (e.g., overall L2 proficiency). Thus, a test measures how *well* someone can do something. In contrast, questionnaires do not have good or bad answers; they ask for information about the respondents (or 'informants') in a non-evaluative manner, without gauging their performance against a set of criteria or against the performance of a norm group. Thus, although some commercially available questionnaires are actually called 'tests,' these are not tests in the same sense as achievement or aptitude tests.

'Production questionnaires' (DCTs) are not questionnaires

The term *'production questionnaire'* is a relatively new name for a popular instrument – traditionally referred to as a DCT or 'discourse completion task' – that has been the most commonly used elicitation technique in the field of interlanguage pragmatics (cf. Bardovi-Harlig, 1999; Johnston, Kasper & Ross, 1998). Although several versions exist, the common feature of production questionnaires is that they require the informant to produce some sort of authentic language data as a response to situational prompts. For example:

```
Rushing to get to class on time, you run round
the corner and bump into one of your fellow stu-
dents who was waiting there, almost knocking him
down.
You: _ _ _ _ _ _ _ _ _ _ _ _ _ _ _ _ _ _ _ _ _ _ _
The student: Never mind, no damage done.
```

(Johnston et al., 1998, p. 176).

It is clear that these 'questionnaires' are not questionnaires in the same psychometric sense as the instruments discussed in this book. They are written, structured language elicitation instruments and, as such, they sample the respondent's competence in performing certain tasks, which makes them similar to language tests.

1.1.2 What do questionnaires measure?

Broadly speaking, questionnaires can yield three types of data about the respondent: *factual, behavioral,* and *attitudinal.*

1. *Factual questions* (also called 'classification' questions or 'subject descriptors') are used to find out about who the respondents are. They typically cover demographic characteristics (e.g., age, gender, and race), residential location, marital and socioeconomic status, level of education, religion, occupation, as well as any other background information that may be relevant to interpreting the findings of the survey. Such additional data in L2 studies often include facts about the learners' language learning history, amount of time spent in an L2 environment, level of parents' L2 proficiency, or the L2 coursebook used.

2. *Behavioral questions* are used to find out what the respondents are doing or have done in the past. They typically ask about people's actions, life-styles, habits, and personal history. Perhaps the most well-known questions of this type in L2 studies are the items in language learning strategy inventories that ask about the frequency one has used a particular strategy in the past.

3. *Attitudinal questions* are used to find out what people think. This is a broad category that concerns *attitudes, opinions, beliefs, interests,* and *values.* These five interrelated terms are not always distinguished or defined very clearly in the literature.

   - *Attitudes* concern evaluative responses to a particular target (e.g., people, institution, situation). They are deeply embedded in the human mind, and are very often not the product of rational deliberation of facts – they can be rooted back in our past or modeled by certain significant people around us. For this reason, they are rather pervasive and resistant to change.

- *Opinions* are just as subjective as attitudes, but they are perceived as being more factually based and more changeable. People are always aware of their opinions but they may not be fully conscious of their attitudes (Aiken, 1996).

- *Beliefs* have a stronger factual support than opinions and often concern the question as to whether something is true, false, or 'right'.

- *Interests* are preferences for particular activities.

- *Values* on the one hand concern preferences for 'life goals' and 'ways of life' (e.g., Christian values); on the other hand they are also used to describe the utility, importance, or worth attached to particular activities, concepts, or objects (e.g., instrumental/utilitarian value of L2 proficiency).

1.2 WHY USE QUESTIONNAIRES AND WHY NOT?

1.2.1 Advantages

The main attraction of questionnaires is their unprecedented efficiency in terms of (a) researcher time, (b) researcher effort, and (c) financial resources. By administering a questionnaire to a group of people, one can collect a huge amount of information in less than an hour, and the personal investment required will be a fraction of what would have been needed for, say, interviewing the same number of people. Furthermore, if the questionnaire is well constructed, processing the data can also be fast and relatively straightforward, especially by using some modern computer software. These cost-benefit considerations are very important, particularly for all those who are doing research in addition to having a full-time job (Gillham, 2000).

Cost-effectiveness is not the only advantage of questionnaires. They are also very *versatile*, which means that they can be used successfully with a variety of people in a variety of situations targeting a variety of topics. As a result, the vast majority of research projects in the behavioral and social sciences involve at one stage or another collecting some sort of questionnaire data.

1.2.2 Disadvantages

Although the previous description of the virtues of questionnaires might suggest that they are perfect research instruments, this is not quite so. Questionnaires have some serious limitations, and some of these have led certain researchers to claim that questionnaire data are not reliable or valid. I do not agree with this claim in general, but there is no doubt that it is very easy to produce unreliable and invalid data by means of ill-constructed questionnaires. In fact, as Gillham (2000, p. 1) points out, in research methodology "no single method has been so much abused." Let us look at the various problem sources.

Simplicity and superficiality of answers

Because respondents are left to their own devices when filling in self-completed questionnaires, the questions need to be sufficiently simple and straightforward to be understood by everybody. Thus, this method is unsuitable for probing deeply into an issue (Moser & Kalton, 1971) and it results in rather superficial data. The necessary simplicity of the questions is further augmented by the fact that the amount of time respondents are usually willing to spend working on a questionnaire is rather short, which again limits the depth of the investigation.

Unreliable and unmotivated respondents

Most people are not very thorough in a research sense, and this is all the more true about dealing with questionnaires – an activity which typically they do not enjoy or benefit from in any way. Thus, the results may vary greatly from one individual to another, depending on the time and care they choose or are able to give (Hopkins, Stanley, & Hopkins, 1990). Respondents are also prone to leave out some questions, either by mistake or because they did not like them, and Low (1999) presents empirical evidence that respondents also often simply misread or misinterpret questions (which of course renders the answers false). If returning the questionnaires to the survey administrator is left to the respondents (for example in a mail survey), they very often fail to do so, even when they have completed it. In such 'distant' modes, the majority of the respondents may not even bother to have a go at the questionnaire. After all, don't we all think, from time to time, that the questionnaires we receive are an absolute nuisance...?

Respondent literacy problems

Questionnaire research makes the inherent assumption that the respondents can read and write well. Even in the industrialized world this is not necessarily the case with regard to the whole population: Statistics of about 5%-7% are regularly quoted when estimating the proportion of people who have difficulty reading, and the number of those who are uncomfortable with writing is even bigger. It is therefore understandable that for respondents with literacy problems, filling in a questionnaire can appear an intimidating or overwhelming task.

Little or no opportunity to correct the respondents' mistakes

Questionnaire items focus on information which the respondents know best, and therefore the researcher has little opportunity to double-check the validity of the answers. Sometimes respondents deviate from the truth intentionally (see further) but it is also common that – as just mentioned – they simply misunderstand or forget something, or do not remember it correctly. Another fairly common situation is when informants do not know the exact response to a question yet answer it without indicating their lack of knowledge. Without any personal contact between the researcher and the informant, little can be done to check the seriousness of the answers and to correct the erroneous responses.

Social desirability (or prestige) bias

The final big problem with regard to questionnaires is that people do not always provide true answers about themselves; that is, the results represent what the respondents *report* to feel or believe, rather than what they *actually* feel or believe. There are several possible reasons for this, and the most salient one is what is usually termed the *social desirability* or *prestige bias*. Questionnaire items are often 'transparent,' that is, respondents can have a fairly good guess about what the desirable/acceptable/expected answer is, and some of them will provide this response even if it is not true. The most extreme example of a 'transparent' question I have come across was in the official U.S. visa application form (OF 156):

"Have you ever participated in genocide?"

Although most questionnaire items are more subtle than this, trying to present ourselves in a good light is a natural human tendency, and this is very bad news for the survey researcher: The resulting bias poses a serious threat to the validity of the data. We should note that this threat is not necessarily confined to 'subjective' attitudinal items only. As Oppenheim (1992) warns us, even factual questions are often loaded with prestige: people might claim that they read more than they do, bathe more often than is true, spend more time with their children, or give more to charity than actually happens, etc. In general, questions concerning age, race, income, state of health, marital status, educational background, sporting achievements, social standing, criminal behavior, sexual activity, and bad habits such as smoking or drinking, are all vulnerable (Newell, 1993; Wilson & McClean, 1994).

Self-deception

Self-deception is related to social desirability but in this case respondents do not deviate from the truth consciously but rather because they also deceive themselves (and not just the researcher). As Hopkins et al. (1990, p. 312) point out, human defense mechanisms "cushion failures, minimize faults, and maximize virtues so that we maintain a sense of personal worth." People with personality problems might simply be unable to give an accurate self-description, but the problem of self-delusion may be present on a more general scale, though to a lesser degree, affecting many other people.

Acquiescence bias

Another common threat inherent to self-completed questionnaires is *acquiescence*, which refers to the tendency for people to agree with sentences when they are unsure or ambivalent. Acquiescent people include "yeasayers," who are ready to go along with "anything that sounds good" (Robinson, Shaver, & Wrightsman, 1991, p. 8), and the term also covers those who are reluctant to look at the negative side of any issue and are unwilling to provide strong negative responses.

Halo effect

The *halo effect* concerns the human tendency to overgeneralize. If our overall impression of a person or a topic is positive, we may be disinclined to say anything less than positive about them even if it comes to specific details. For many students, for example, a teacher they love is 'perfect' in everything he/she does – which is obviously not true. And similarly, if we do not like someone, we – quite unfairly – tend to underestimate all his/her characteristics.

Fatigue effects

Finally, if a questionnaire is too long or monotonous, respondents may begin to respond inaccurately as a result of tiredness or boredom. This effect is called the *fatigue effect*, and it is obviously more likely to influence responses toward the end of the questionnaire.

1.3 QUESTIONNAIRES IN QUANTITATIVE AND QUALITATIVE RESEARCH

The typical questionnaire is a highly structured data collection instrument, with most items either asking about very specific pieces of information (e.g., one's address or food preference) or giving various response options for the respondent to choose from, for example by ticking a box. This makes questionnaire data particularly suited for *quantitative*, statistical analysis. After all, the essential characteristic of quantitative research is that it employs categories, viewpoints, and models that have been precisely defined by the researcher in advance, and numerical or directly quantifiable data are collected to determine the relationship between these categories and to test the research hypotheses.

In theory, it would be possible to devise a questionnaire that is entirely made up of truly open-ended items (e.g., "Describe your dreams for the future..."). Such an instrument would provide data that are *qualitative* and *exploratory* in nature, but this practice is usually discouraged by theoreticians. The problem with questionnaires from a qualitative perspective is that – as argued earlier – they inherently involve a somewhat superficial and relatively brief engagement with the topic on the part of the respondent. Therefore, no matter how creatively we formulate the items, they are unlikely to yield the kind of rich and sensitive description of events and participant perspectives that qualitative interpretations are grounded in. In fact, as Sudman and Bradburn (1983) assert, requests for long responses (i.e., more than a sentence as a minimum) often lead to refusals to answer the question or the entire questionnaire, and even if we get longer written answers, many of these will need to be discarded because they are uncodable or inappropriate. So, if we are seeking long and detailed personal accounts, other research methods such as a personal interview are likely to be more suitable for our purpose. Having said that, I do believe that some partially open-ended questions can play an important role in questionnaires (see Section 2.5, for a discussion), but if we want to significantly enrich questionnaire data, the most effective strategy is usually not the inclusion of too many open-ended questions but to combine the questionnaire survey with other data collection procedures (see Section 4.7).

True...

"The desire to use open-ended questions appears to be almost universal in novice researchers, but is usually rapidly extinguished with experience."

(Robson, 1993, p. 243)

2
Constructing the Questionnaire

Section 1.2.2 contained a long list of potential problems with self-completed questionnaires. My goal was not to dissuade people from using such instruments but rather to raise awareness of these possible shortcomings. It is true that respondents are often unmotivated, slapdash, hasty, and insincere, yet it is also an established fact that careful and creative questionnaire construction can result in an instrument that motivates people to give relatively truthful and thoughtful answers, which can then be processed in a scientifically sound manner. The relevant professional literature contains a significant body of accumulated experience and research evidence as to how we can achieve this. Some of the points highlighted by researchers are seemingly trivial in the sense that they concern small details, but I have come to believe that it is to a great extent the systematic handling of such small details and nuances that will eventually turn an *ad hoc* set of questions into an effective research instrument.

I agree...

"Questionnaires can be designed to minimize, but not eliminate, dishonest, and careless reporting."

(Aiken, 1997, p. 58)

Constructing a good questionnaires involves a series of steps and procedures, including:

- Deciding on the general features of the questionnaire, such as the length, the format, and the main parts.
- Writing effective items/questions and drawing up an item pool.

16

- Selecting and sequencing the items.
- Writing appropriate instructions and examples.
- Piloting the questionnaire and conducting item analysis.

This chapter will provide an overview of these issues, offering many practical do's and don'ts to facilitate effective questionnaire construction.

Indeed...

"Questionnaires are so easy to do quickly and badly that, in a way, they invite carelessness."

(Gillham, 2000, p. 11)

2.1 GENERAL FEATURES

Between the initial idea of preparing a questionnaire for the purpose of our research and actually getting down to writing the first draft, a number of important decisions need to be taken regarding the general features of the would-be instrument. First of all, we need to specify the maximum *length of time* that the completion of the questionnaire could take; then we need to consider general *format characteristics*; and finally we need to think about the issue of *anonymity*, particularly if we are going to target sensitive/confidential topics.

2.1.1 Length

When we design a questionnaire, the general temptation is always to cover too much ground by asking everything that might turn out to be interesting. This must be resisted: in questionnaire design less is often more because long questionnaires can become counterproductive.

How long is the optimal length? It depends on how important the topic of the questionnaire is for the respondent. If we feel very strongly about something, we are usually willing to spend several hours answering questions. However, most questionnaires in the L2 field concern topics that have a low salience from the respondents' perspective, and in such cases the optimal length is rather short. Most researchers agree that anything that is more than 4-6 pages long and requires over half an hour to complete may be considered too much of an imposition. As a principle, I have always tried to stay within a 4-page limit: It is remarkable how many items can be included within 4 well-designed pages and I have also found that a questionnaire of 3-4 pages does not tend to exceed the 30-minute completion limit.

A further factor to consider is that if we are restricted in the time we can have access to the respondents, for example when we administer a questionnaire to learners during their teaching hours, the maximum length should be set with the slowest readers in mind. For example, in a national survey that involved the group-administration of a questionnaire in hundreds of primary school classes in various locations in Hungary (Dörnyei & Clément, 2001; Dörnyei & Csizér, in press), we could only negotiate a maximum of 30 minutes' access to the children. This meant that the questionnaire had to be cut down to three pages and an estimated 20-minute completion time in order to give everybody a chance to finish within the allotted time.

To summarize

In my experience, only in exceptional cases should a questionnaire:

- be more than 4 pages long;
- take more than 30 minutes to complete.

2.1.2 Layout

Sanchez (1992) points out that the design of the *questionnaire layout* is frequently overlooked as an important aspect of the development of the instrument. This is a mistake: Because in surveys employing self-completed questionnaires the main interface between the researcher and the respondent is the hard copy of the questionnaire; the format and graphic layout carry a special significance and have an important impact on the responses. Over the past 15 years I have increasingly come to the belief that producing an attractive and professional design is half the battle in eliciting reliable and valid data (for a discussion of the role of the layout in increasing respondent motivation, see Section 3.3.8).

What does an 'attractive and professional design' involve? The following list summarizes the five most important points:

- *Booklet format.* Not only does the questionnaire have to be short but it also has to *look* short. I have found that the format that feels most compact is that of a *booklet.* It can be achieved by taking a double-sized sheet (A3 size in Europe), photocopying two nor-mal-sized pages on each of the sides, and then folding the sheet into two. This format also makes it easy to read and to turn pages (and what is just as important, it also prevents lost pages…).

- *Appropriate density.* With regard to how much material we put on a page, a compromise needs to be achieved: On the one hand, we want to make the pages full because respondents are much more willing to fill in a two-page rather than a four-page questionnaire even if the two instruments have exactly the same number of items. On the other hand, we must not make the pages look crowded (for example by economizing on the spaces separating different sections of the questionnaire). Effective ways of achiev-ing this trade-off involve reducing the *margins,* using a *space-economical font* (e.g., 11- or 12-point Times New Roman), and utilizing the whole *width* of the page, for example by printing the response options next to the questions and not below (as illus-trated in the following example).

	Strongly disagree	Disagree	Slightly disagree	Partly agree	Agree	Strongly agree
1. Language learning is a burden for me.						
2. Foreign languages are an important part of the school curriculum.						
3. I like the sound of English.						

On length and crowdedness

"Perhaps the most common mistake of the beginner in questionnaire construction is to crowd questions together in the hope of making the questionnaire look short. ... While length is important, the respondent's perception of the difficulty of the task is even more important on self-administered questionnaires. A less crowded questionnaire with substantial white space looks easier and generally results in higher cooperation and fewer errors."

(Sudman & Bradburn, 1983, p. 244)

- *Orderly layout.* Even if the page is dense, a well-designed, orderly layout that utilizes various typefaces and highlighting options (e.g., bold characters or italics) can create a good impression, whereas an unsystematic layout, even if it is more spacious, can appear chaotic. It is also essential that the final version be nicely printed – as Newell (1993) points out, in these days of sophisticated word-processors, people are used to receiving good quality hard copy. So try and find a laser printer and a good photocopier!

- *Paper quality.* Even the quality and color of the paper might make a difference. Newell (1993) describes a colleague who has always produced documents on thick, beige paper because she believes that "(1) it stands out from the mass of other paper which might be received, (2) it is pleasant to handle, and (3) people will not have the heart to throw away such an attractive document. She says it works" (p. 109). Other researchers suggest that it may be useful to separate the various parts of the questionnaires with a certain color-code of the paper used as it clarifies the structure (Robson, 1993); for example, the paper of the cover page or the instructions can be of a different color.

- *Sequence marking.* I normally mark each main section of the questionnaire with Roman numbers, each question with consecutive Arab figures, and then letter all the subparts of a question; as a result, I may have Question 1a or 27d within Section I or III (see the example on page 22). This creates a sense of structuredness. It is also beneficial to include a phrase such as "Continued on back" at the bottom of the first side of a page that is printed on both sides. Finally, it is probably obvious but still worth mentioning that a question should not be split between two pages.

2.1.3 Sensitive topics and anonymity

It was mentioned in Section 1.2.2 that respondents are sometimes reluctant to give honest answers to sensitive questions. Questionnaire items differ greatly in terms of how threatening/imposing/sensitive/ embarrassing they feel. It requires little justification that we need to approach the issue of constructing and administering the questionnaire in a very different way if it concerns, for example, the evaluation of the L2 teacher or the school rather than one's interest in travelling abroad.

Example of sequence marking

I. ATTITUDES TOWARD LANGUAGE LEARNING

    1. Language learning is an exciting activity.
    2. Language learning often makes me happy.

II. LANGUAGE CHOICE

    3. If you could choose, which foreign languages would you choose to learn next year at school? Please mark three languages in order of importance.

    (a) ....

    (b)..

    (c) ....

Continued on back...

Sensitive topics

'Sensitive' topics are not confined to explicitly illegal or embarrassing subjects but also include basic demographic items such as age or marital status. Indeed, various facts of life can carry such a prominent social and emotional loading that questions targeting them often fall prey to the respondents' 'social desirability' bias (cf. Section 1.2.2). Depending on our core values, we are likely to overreport on what we conceive as a positive aspect and underreport on a negative one.

Questionnaire designers need to be aware of this tendency and a good initial rule of thumb is that we should *not* ask any sensitive questions unless absolutely necessary for the project.

In Section 2.6.3, I will discuss several item-writing strategies that might make such questions more palatable, and in Section 3.4 we will look at questionnaire administration techniques that may help to 'sell' these items. Here I would like to highlight the usefulness of an explicit statement or promise of confidentiality in overcoming possible apprehensions. Oppenheim (1992, pp. 104-105) suggests that something along the following line be displayed prominently on the front of the questionnaire:

> THE CONTENTS OF THIS FORM ARE *ABSOLUTELY* CONFIDENTIAL. INFORMATION IDENTIFYING THE RESPONDENT WILL NOT BE DISCLOSED UNDER ANY CIRCUMSTANCES.

In the general instructions of a motivation questionnaire among school learners which included the appraisal of the L2 teacher and course (and was therefore particularly sensitive from the students' point of view), Gliksman, Gardner and Smythe (1982, p. 637) provided the following detailed description of how confidentiality was observed in spite of asking the students to state their names:

> Your answers to any or all questions will be treated with the strictest confidence. Although we ask for your name on the cover page, we do so only because we must be able to associate your answers to this questionnaire with those of other questionnaires which you will be asked to answer. It is important for you to know, however, that before the questionnaires are examined, your questionnaire will be numbered, the same number will be put on the section containing your name, and then that section will be removed. By following a similar procedure with the other questionnaires we will be able to match the questionnaires through matching numbers and avoid having to associate your name directly with the questionnaire.

Anonymity

One frequent method used to diffuse sensitive items is to make the questionnaire *anonymous*. For example, in a student questionnaire that asked the learners to evaluate their language teacher and the course (Clément, Dörnyei, & Noels, 1994), using similar items to the ones employed in the Gliksman et al. (1982) study just mentioned, we felt it unlikely that the 16/17-year-old teenagers in the sample were going to agree to give us honest answers without being assured about the anonymity of the questionnaires. Following the same reasoning – and particularly when legal considerations, such as local research regulations, also necessitate it – researchers often feel 'forced' to make the survey anonymous. The main argument to support this practice is that anonymous respondents are likely to give answers that are less self-protective and presumably more accurate than respondents who believe they can be identified (Kearney, Hopkins, Mauss and Weisheit, 1984). Anonymity, however, raises two issues:

- Opinions differ widely as to whether respondent anonymity actually fulfills its purpose in encouraging honesty and willingness to disclose. As Aiken (1997) summarizes, most adults will probably give the same answers to questionnaire items whether or not their responses are anonymous. For example, Sudman and Bradburn (1983) report on a large-scale postal survey of college graduates, in which the researchers placed the mailing label (which naturally contained the respondent's name) on the back cover of the questionnaires and sent these out in window envelopes. Out of the 40,000 recipients, only five objected to this procedure and scratched out their names. On the other hand, in situations when an honest answer might cause embarrassment or pose actual threat to the respondent, anonymity does obviously matter. Thus, the question to consider is whether our questionnaires really falls into this category.

- Anonymity may not serve the purpose of the investigation. More often than not the researcher would like to link the data from the questionnaires to data coming from other sources; for example, motivational data obtained by questionnaires is often correlated to achievement scores coming from end-of-term course grades or proficiency tests. Without any identity marking on the question-naires, we simply cannot link someone's scores in the two da-tasets. Similarly, if we are conducting a longitudinal investigation we would not be able to follow a person's development if all the answers gathered from the multiple subjects at a time were anonymous.

In sum, sensitive items and anonymity are a serious issue that needs to be considered right from the beginning. In Section 3.4.3, I will present some approaches that have been successfully used in the past to reconcile confidentiality with the need for identification for re-search purposes.

2.2 THE MAIN PARTS OF A QUESTIONNAIRE

Bearing in mind the general considerations just discussed, we are now set to start drawing up the first draft of the questionnaire. Before we get down to describing the various item types, let me briefly summa-rize the main components of a questionnaire.

2.2.1 Title

Just like any other piece of writing, a questionnaire should have a title to identify the domain of the investigation, to provide the respondent with initial orientation, and to activate various content schemata. Be-cause uninformative titles fail to achieve these objectives, Aiken (1997) suggests that we should try and avoid title words like "ques-tionnaire" or "survey." For better identification, the title might be accompanied by the date of the survey administration and the name of the organization conducting or sponsoring the study.

2.2.2 Instructions

The title of the questionnaire is followed by instructions. These cannot be too long and yet need to be informative and well pitched because they play an important role in determining the respondents' feelings toward the questionnaire and in specifying how they should go about answering the items. Instructions are of two types:

- *General instruction* (or 'opening greeting') at the beginning of the questionnaire.
- *Specific instructions* introducing each new task.

General instruction

As a minimum, the general instruction (or 'opening greeting') should cover the following points (see also Section 3.2.1, for special instructions for mail surveys):

- What the study is about and why it is important or socially useful.
- The organization responsible for conducting the study.
- Emphasizing that there are no right or wrong answers; requesting honest answers and trying to elicit integrity in general.
- Promising confidentiality.
- Saying 'thank you.'

For better readability and emphasis, the instructions should be graphically highlighted, such as being printed in boldface type, and the main pieces of information can also be given in a format such as bulleted points. I would expect the following sample instruction would be suitable for most purposes.

Sample 2.1. General instruction

We would like to ask you to help us by answering the following questions concerning foreign language learning. This survey is conducted by the Language Research Group of the University of X to better understand... This is not a test so there are no "right" or "wrong" answers and you don't even have to write your name on it. We are interested in your personal opinion. Please give your answers sincerely as only this will guarantee the success of the investigation. Thank you very much for your help.

Specific instructions

Specific instructions explain and demonstrate how respondents should go about answering the questions. It is obvious that this is a crucial part. Each new task-type requires instructions, and in order to separate these instructions from the rest of the text, they should be graphically highlighted, for example by printing them in bold (just like the general instruction).

A very important role of the instructions is to explain how various rating scales (cf. Section 2.4.1) work and what the various rating criteria are. For example, if we ask the respondents to produce evaluations on a five-point scale (i.e., giving marks ranging from 1 to 5), we needs to explain very clearly what each numerical category stands for. Then, to avoid misunderstandings and mistakes, a short summary of this explanation will need to be repeated at least twice on each new page. Samples 2.2 and 2.3 on pages 28-29 provide examples of instructions for two common rating scale types (see also, Sample 2.4 on page 41).

Sample 2.2. Instructions for numerical rating scales

In the following section we would like you to answer some questions by simply giving marks from 1 to 5.

1 = not at all   2 = not really   3 = so-so   4 = quite a lot   5 = very much

For example, consider the following item. If you like hamburgers very much, write '5' in the space in front of the question:

_____ How much do you like hamburgers?

Please write one (and only one) whole number in front of each question and don't leave out any of them. Thanks.

2.2.3 Questionnaire items

After the instructions comes the central part of the questionnaire, the actual items. They will be discussed in detail in Sections 2.3 – 2.7. Two points need to be made here:

- Questionnaire items rarely take the form of actual questions that end with a question mark. The item type found in Sample 2.3, for example, is far more common than that in Sample 2.2 (which is a real question).

- The items need to be very clearly separated from the instructions. This is where different typefaces and font styles come in handy.

Sample 2.3.   Instructions for Likert scales

Following are a number of statements with which some people agree and others disagree. We would like you to indicate your opinion after each statement by putting an 'X' in the box that best indicates the extent to which you agree or disagree with the statement. Thank you very much for your help.

For example:

Pickled cucumbers are unhealthy.

☐	☐	☐	☐	☐	☐
Strongly disagree	Disagree	Slightly disagree	Partly agree	Agree	Strongly agree

If you think, for example, that there is something true about this statement but it is somewhat exaggerated, you can put an 'X' in the fourth or the fifth box.

2.2.4 Additional information

Depending on circumstances, the questionnaire may contain, usually at the end, a short additional information section in which the author can address the respondent concerning a number of issues:

- Unless the researcher or a representative is present during the completion of the questionnaire, it might be worth including a contact name (e.g., the researcher's or an administrator's) with a telephone number or address and some explicit encouragement to get in touch if there are any questions.

- In 'distant' situations, it might also be worth summarizing briefly how the questionnaires should be returned, and even when a return envelope is provided, we should print on the questionnaire the name and the address of the person to whom the completed questionnaire is to be sent.

- It is a nice gesture (unfortunately too rarely used) to include a brief note promising to send the respondent a summary of the findings if interested (see Section 3.3.9, for a discussion of this point).

- Sometimes questionnaires can also end with an invitation to volunteer for a follow-up interview.

2.2.5 Final 'thank you'

It is basic courtesy, yet it is all too often overlooked, that the respondents should be thanked for their cooperation at the very end of the questionnaire. After all, they have done us a favor. Although I usually do not include any drawings in my questionnaires, if I did it would be located here: a smiling face or some little figure that can be seen as a nice gesture. Modern word processing packages offer many graphic designs, such as:

2.3 QUESTIONNAIRE CONTENT AND MULTI-ITEM SCALES

The first step in preparing the questionnaire items is to specify their content in explicit terms. Although this may sound obvious, it does not always happen, and vague content specifications can pose a serious threat to the validity and reliability of the instrument, particularly in two areas:

- the appropriate sampling of the content;
- the preparation of multi-item scales.

2.3.1 Appropriate sampling of the content

Ad hoc questionnaire design involves jotting down a number of relevant questions without any rigorous procedure to ensure that the coverage is comprehensive. The problem with this method, as Davidson (1996, p. 10) highlights, is that "You cannot analyze what you do not measure." That is, not even the most sophisticated data analysis techniques will be able to compensate for leaving out some important questions from the data collection by accident. Certain omissions are bound to occur even in otherwise very thorough studies (as attested by the countless anecdotes one hears at professional conferences) but when the sampling of the content is not theory-driven, the chances for something irrecoverable to happen are obviously much greater.

On the other hand, forewarned by the potential threat of a lack of comprehensiveness, researchers may be tempted to make the questionnaire too long by covering every possible angle. Although this is undesirable, without any explicit content specifications it is almost impossible to decide what limit to put on the range of questions. So, the initial stage of questionnaire design should focus on clarifying the research problem and identifying what critical concepts need to be addressed by the questionnaire. To facilitate this, it is often recommended that the questionnaire design phase be preceded by a small-scale qualitative study (e.g., focus group interviews) to provide information on the relevant points and issues.

Yes!

"The temptation is always to cover too much, to ask everything that might turn out to be interesting. This must be resisted."

(Moser & Kalton, 1971, p. 309)

Once a theoretically sound shortlist of specific content areas has been drawn up, it becomes possible to eliminate all the questions that are only of peripheral interest but not directly related to the variables and hypotheses that the questionnaire has been designed to investigate. Such a shortlist is also necessary to be able to produce 'multi-item scales' (see below), without which no questionnaire can be reliable.

To illustrate this process, let us take a concrete example: the design of a short questionnaire to assess student attitudes toward the language teacher. Which aspects of the teacher shall we concentrate on? Without any theoretical guidelines we could be producing an infinite number of items, all seemingly targeting important teacher characteristics. In a study where we faced this problem (Clément et al., 1994), in order to follow a more systematic approach we first conducted a review of the relevant literature and identified four main dimensions of teacher appraisal: *competence, rapport* (with the students), *motivation,* and *teaching style/personality.* We then used this list to guide us in generating the item pool.

2.3.2 Using multi-item scales

Multi-item scales are the key components to scientific questionnaire design, yet this concept is surprisingly little known in the L2 profession. The core of the issue is that when it comes to assessing attitudes, beliefs, opinions, interests, values, aspirations, expectations, and other personal variables, the actual wording of the questions assumes an unexpected importance: minor differences in how the question is formulated and framed can produce radically different levels of agreement or disagreement, or a completely different selection of answers (Gillham, 2000). We do not have such problems with factual questions: if you are interested in the gender of the respondent, you can safely ask about this using a single item, and the chances are that you will get a reliable answer (although the item: *"Your sex:"* might elicit very creative responses in a teenage sample...). However, with non-factual answers it is not unusual to find that responses given by the same people to two virtually identical items differ by as much as 20% or more (Oppenheim, 1992). Here is an illustration:

Converse & Presser (1986, p. 41) report on a case when simply changing "forbid" to "not allow" in the wording produced significantly different responses in the item *"Do you think the United States should [forbid/not allow] public speeches against democracy?"* Significantly more people were willing to "not allow" speeches against democracy than were willing to "forbid" them. Although it may be true that on an impressionistic level "not allow" somehow does not sound as harsh as "forbid," the fact is that 'allow' and 'forbid' are exact logical opposites and therefore it was not unreasonable to assume that the actual content of the two versions of the question was identical. Yet, as the differing response pattern indicated, this was not the case. Given that in this example only one word was changed and that the alternative version had an almost identical meaning, this is a good illustration that item wording in general has a substantial impact on the responses. However, there does not seem to be a reliable way of knowing exactly what kind of an effect to expect.

So what is the solution? Do we have to conclude that questionnaires simply cannot achieve the kind of accuracy that is needed for scientific measurement purposes? We would have to if measurement theoreticians – and particularly Rensis Likert in the 1930s – had not discovered an ingenious way of getting around the problem: by using *multi-item scales*. These scales refer to a cluster of several differently worded items that focus on the same target (e.g., five items targeting attitudes toward language labs). The item scores for the similar questions are summed, resulting in a total scale score (which is why these scales are sometimes referred to as *summative scales*), and the underlying assumption is that any idiosyncratic interpretation of an item will be averaged out during the summation of the item scores. In other words, if we use multi-item scales, "no individual item carries an excessive load, and an inconsistent response to one item would cause limited damage" (Skehan, 1989, p. 11). For example, the question "Do you learn vocabulary items easily?" is bound to be interpreted differently by different people, depending on how easy they consider 'easily,' but if we include several more items asking about how good the respondents' memorization skills are, the overall score is likely to reflect the actual level of the development of this skill. Thus, multi-item scales maximize the stable component that the items share and reduce the extraneous influences unique to the individual items.

A problem indeed...

"When we sometimes despair about the use of language as a tool for measuring or at least uncovering awareness, attitude, percepts and belief systems, it is mainly because we do not yet know *why* questions that look so similar actually produce such very different sets of results, or how we can predict contextual effects on a question, or in what ways we can ensure that respondents will all use the same frame of reference in answering an attitude question."

(Oppenheim, 1992, p. 149)

Because of the fallibility of single items, there is a general consensus among survey specialists that more than one item is needed to address each identified content area, all aimed at the same target but drawing upon slightly different aspects of it. How many is 'more than one'? The most well-known standardized questionnaire in the L2 field, Robert Gardner's (1985) Attitude/Motivation Test Battery (AMTB), contains 4-10 items to measure each scale. It is rather risky to go below 4 items per subarea because if the *post hoc* item analysis (cf. Section 2.9.3) reveals that certain items did not work in the particular sample, their exclusion will result in too short (or single-item) scales. The technicalities of how to produce reliable and valid multi-item scales will be discussed in the section on "rating scales" (Section 2.4.1).

Of course, nothing is perfect. While multi-item scales do a good job in terms of psychometric reliability, they may not necessarily appeal to the respondents. Ellard and Rogers (1993) report that respondents sometimes react negatively to items that appear to be asking the same question because this gives them the impression that we are trying to "trick them or check their honesty" (p. 19). This problem, however, can be greatly reduced by using effective item-writing strategies (see Section 2.6, for a summary).

2.4 'CLOSED-ENDED' QUESTIONNAIRE ITEMS

Let us start our exploration of the various types of questionnaire items by first examining the most frequent question type: *closed-ended* (or simply *'closed'*) *questions*. Although this category subsumes several very different item types, these all share in common the fact that the respondent is provided with ready-made response options to choose from, normally by encircling or ticking one of them or by putting an 'X' in the appropriate slot/box. That is, these items do not require the respondents to produce any free writing; instead, they are to choose one of the alternatives, regardless of whether their preferred answer is among them.

The major advantage of closed-ended questions is that their coding and tabulation is straightforward and leaves no room for rater subjectivity. Accordingly, these questions are sometimes referred to as 'objective' items. They are particularly suited for quantitative, statistical analyses (cf. Section 4.3) because the response options can easily be numerically coded and entered into a computer database.

2.4.1 Rating scales

Ratings scales are undoubtedly the most popular items in research questionnaires. They require the respondent to make an evaluative judgement of the target by marking one of a series of categories organized into a *scale*. (Note that the term 'scale' has, unfortunately, two meanings in measurement theory: one referring to a cluster of items measuring the same thing – cf. Section 2.3.2 on 'multi-item scales' – and the other, discussed in this section, referring to a measurement procedure utilizing an ordered series of response categories.) The various points on the continuum of the scale indicate different degrees of a certain category; this can be of a diverse nature, ranging from various attributes (e.g., frequency or quality) to intensity (e.g., very much → not at all) and opinion (e.g., strongly agree → strongly disagree). The points on the scale are subsequently assigned successive numbers, which makes their computer coding a simple task.

The big asset of rating scales is that they can be used for evaluating almost anything, and accordingly, as Aiken (1996) points out, these scales are second only to teacher-made achievement tests in the frequency of usage of all psychological measurement procedures. Indeed, I believe that few people in the teaching profession are unfamiliar with this item format: we are regularly asked to complete rating scales in various evaluation forms (of students, teachers, coursebooks, or courses), and outside the school context we also frequently come across them, for example when asked about our opinions of certain services (e.g., in hotels, transport).

Likert scales

The most commonly used scaling technique is the *Likert scale*, which has been named after its inventor, Rensis Likert. Over the past 70 years (Likert's original article came out in 1932) the number of research studies employing this technique has certainly reached a six-digit figure, which is due to the fact that the method is simple, versatile, and reliable.

Likert scales consist of a series of statements all of which are related to a particular target (which can be, among others, an individual person, a group of people, an institution, or a concept); respondents are asked to indicate the extent to which they agree or disagree with these items by marking (e.g., circling) one of the responses ranging from 'strongly agree' to 'strongly disagree.' For example:

Hungarians are genuinely nice people.

Strongly   Agree   Neither agree   Disagree   Strongly
  agree   nor disagree   disagree

After the scale has been administered, each response option is assigned a number for scoring purposes (e.g., 'strongly agree' = 5, 'strongly disagree' = 1). With negatively worded items the scores are usually reversed before analysis. Finally, the scores for the items addressing the same target are summed up or averaged. Thus, Likert scales are multi-item scales, following a 'summative model.'

The statements on Likert scales should be 'characteristic,' that is, expressing either a positive/favorable or a negative/unfavorable attitude toward the object of interest. Neutral items (e.g., *"I think Hungarians are all right"*) do not work well on a Likert scale because they do not evoke salient evaluative reactions, and extreme items are also to be avoided. An important concern of questionnaire designers is to decide the *number of steps* or response options each scale contains. Original Likert scales contained five response options (as just illustrated), but subsequent research has also used two-, three-, four-, six-, and seven-response options successfully. The most common step numbers have been five or six, which raises a second important questions: Shall we use an even or an odd number of steps?

Some researchers prefer using an even number of response options because of the concern that certain respondents might use the middle category ('neither agree nor disagree,' 'not sure,' or 'neutral') to avoid making a real choice, that is, to take the easy way out. Although according to research, this may be true of roughly 20% of the respondents, it appears that the inclusion or exclusion of a middle category does not affect the *relative* proportions of those actually expressing opinions and thus does not modify the results significantly (Nunnally, 1978; Robson, 1993). My personal preference in the past has been to omit the 'undecided' category and to use a six-point scale such as the one illustrated in Sample 2.3 (on page 29).

The final question regarding Likert scales concerns the format of the respondents' answers: How do various physical appearances such as encircling options or ticking boxes compare to each other? Nunnally (1978) states that such variations appear to make little difference in the important psychometric properties of ratings as long as the layout of the questionnaire is clear and there are sufficient instructions and examples to orientate the respondents.

Likert scales have been used successfully with younger children as well; in such cases the number of the response options is often reduced to three and the options themselves are presented in a pictorial format instead of words. For example, in a three-point 'smilegram' children are asked to check the box under the face that best expresses how they feel toward a target:

Variations on Likert scales

Likert scales use response options representing the degree of agreement. This standard set of responses (i.e., strongly agree → strongly disagree) can be easily replaced by other descriptive terms that are relevant to the target. For example, Oxford's (1990) "Strategy Inventory in Language Learning" uses categories ranging from 'Never or almost never true of me' to 'Always or almost always true of me.' Or, in Dörnyei and Clément's (2001) "Language Orientation Questionnaire" a five-point scale ranging from "Not at all true" to "Absolutely true" has been used to assess attitudes toward language learning.

While these variations usually work well, we need to be careful about how to aggregate item scores to obtain multi-item scale scores. Likert scale items that measure the same attitude can simply be summed up because they refer to the same target and it is assumed that a higher total score reflects a stronger endorsement of the target attitude. However, not every variation on Likert scales is summative in the psychometric sense. For example, in Oxford's (1990) learning strategy inventory just mentioned, the various items within a group ask about the frequency of the use of different strategies. In this case, summing up the items would imply that the more strategies a person uses, the more developed his/her strategic skills are in the particular area. However, with regard to learning strategies this is *not* the case, since it is the *quality* rather than the quantity of the strategies a person utilizes that matters: One can be a very competent strategy user by consistently employing one single strategy that particularly suits his/her abilities and learning style. Thus, in this case, the summation of different item scores is not related linearly to the underlying trait.

Semantic differential scales

Instead of Likert scales we can also use *semantic differential scales* for certain measurement purposes. These are very useful in that by using them we can avoid writing statements (which is not always easy); instead, respondents are asked to indicate their answers by marking a continuum (with a tick or an 'X') between two bipolar adjectives on the extremes. For example:

```
Listening comprehension tasks are:

difficult ___:___:___:___:___: X :___ easy

useless  ___: X :___:___:___:___:___ useful
```

These scales are based on the recognition that most adjectives have logical opposites and where an opposing adjective is not obviously available, one can easily be generated with 'in-' or 'un-' or by simply writing 'not ...'. Although the scope of semantic differential scales is more limited than that of Likert scales, the ease of their construction and the fact that the method is easily adaptable to study virtually any concept, activity, or person, may compensate for this. Oppenheim (1992) raises an interesting point concerning the content of semantic differential scales. He argues that it is possible and often useful to include adjective pairs that are seemingly inappropriate to the concept under consideration, such as masculine/feminine (with respect to a brand of cigarettes, for example), or rough/smooth (with respect to, say, Socialism): "By their more imaginative approach, such scales can be used to cover aspects that respondents can hardly put into words, though they do reflect an attitude or feeling" (p. 239). An additional bonus of semantic differential scales is that because they involve little reading, very little testing time is required.

Semantic differential scales are similar to Likert scales in that several items are used to evaluate the same target, and multi-item scores are computed by summing up the individual item scores. An important technical point concerning the construction of such bipolar scales is that the position of the 'negative' and 'positive' poles, if they can be designated as such, should be varied (i.e., the positive pole should alternate between being on the right and the left sides) to avoid superficial responding or a position response set (Aiken, 1996).

Semantic differential scales have been around for almost 50 years and during this time several factor analytic studies examined their content structure. The general conclusion is that there are three major factors of meaning involved in them:

- *evaluation*, referring to the overall positive meaning associated with the target (e.g., good-bad, wise-foolish, honest-dishonest);

- *potency*, referring to the target's overall strength or importance (e.g., strong-weak, hard-soft, useful-useless);

- *activity*, referring to the extent to which the target is associated with action (active-passive, tense-relaxed, quick-slow).

Scales are normally constructed to contain items focusing on each of the three dimensions; however, the items measuring the three evaluative aspects tend to correlate with each other.

Sample 2.4 Instructions for semantic differential scales

The following section of the questionnaire aims at finding out about your ideas and impressions about SOMETHING. In answering the questions we would like to ask you to rate these concepts on a number of scales. These all have pairs of opposites at each end, and between these there are 7 dashes. You are to place a check mark on one of the seven positions, indicating how you feel about the particular concept in view of the two poles. For example, if the scales refer to "listening comprehension tasks" and you find these rather useless and fairly easy, you can place your check marks as follows:

LISTENING COMPREHENSION TASKS ARE:

difficult ___:___:___:___:___: X :___ easy

useless ___: X :___:___:___:___:___ useful

In the following items please place your check marks rapidly and don't stop to think about each scale. We are interested in your immediate impression. Remember, this is not a test and there are no right or wrong answers. The "right" answer is the one that is true for you. Be sure to make only one check mark on each scale. Thank you!

Numerical rating scales

Teenagers sometimes play a rating game whereby they evaluate the appearance and 'sexiness' of the various girls/boys they see passing by in the street on a scale of 1-10. They would be surprised to hear that what they are doing is applying *numerical rating scales*. These scales involve 'giving so many marks out of so many,' that is, assigning one of several numbers corresponding to a series of ordered categories describing a feature of the target. The popularity of this scaling technique is due to the fact that the rating continuum can refer to a wide range of adjectives (e.g., excellent → poor; conscientious → slapdash) or adverbs (e.g., always → never); in fact, numerical ratings can easily be turned into semantic differential scales and vice versa. Sample 2.2 on page 28 provides an example.

True-false items

In some scales the designers only set two response options: true versus false (or 'yes' or 'no'), resulting in what is usually referred to as a *'true-false item.'* While generally it is true that the more options an item contains, the more accurate evaluation it yields, there might be cases when only such a polarized, yes-no decision can be considered reliable. For example, little children are sometimes seen as incapable of providing more elaborate ratings, and some personality test items also follow a true-false rating to ensure reliability in domains where the respondent may not be able to properly evaluate the degree to which a particular feature is present/true or not. In addition, with certain specific areas such as study habits, it may also be more appropriate to apply true/false items when the questions ask about occurrences of various behaviors in the past.

The key sentence (i.e., the one to be judged) in a good true-false item is relatively short and contains a single idea that is not subject to debate (i.e., it is either true or false). Due to the nature of the responses, the *acquiescence bias* (cf. Section 1.2.2) – that is, the tendency to respond in the affirmative direction when in doubt – may be a problem (Aiken, 1997). Because offering a polarized, black-and-white judgment can often be perceived as too forced, some scales include a middle position, involving an 'undecided,' 'neutral,' or 'don't know' option.

2.4.2 Multiple-choice items

Language researchers will be very familiar with the multiple-choice item format because of its popularity in standardized L2 proficiency testing. The item type is also frequently used in questionnaires with respondents being asked to mark – depending on the question – one or more options. If none of the items apply, the respondent may have the option to leave the question unanswered, but because this makes it difficult to decide later whether the omission of a mark was a conscious decision or just an accident, it is better to include a *"Don't know"* and a *"Not applicable"* category (and sometimes even a *"No response"* option). Also, it is often desirable to ensure that an exhaustive list of categories is provided, and for this purpose it may be necessary to include an *"Other"* category, typically followed by an open-ended question of the *"Please specify"* sort (cf. Section 2.5.2).

Multiple choice items are relatively straightforward. It makes them more reader-friendly if we can make the response options shorter by including as much information in the stem as we can without repeating this every time. It also makes it easier to answer them if the response options have a natural order; otherwise they should be arranged in a random or alphabetical order. It is an obvious yet often violated rule that all options should be grammatically correct with respect to the stem. Finally, the use of negative expressions, such as "not," should be avoided in both the stem and the response options – a rule that generally applies to all question types (cf. Section 2.6.2).

Interestingly, multiple-choice items can also produce ordinal rather than nominal (categorical) data (cf. Section 4.3.4), that is, the various alternatives can represent *degrees* of an attitude, interest, and belief. Respondents are, then, instructed to choose only one of these options and their answers will be coded according to the value of the particular option they chose: e.g., Option A may be assigned '2' and Option D '3'. Obviously the value of each option cannot be set in advance on a purely theoretical basis but can only be deduced from extensive pilot testing (cf. Section 2.9) whereby the items are administered to a group of respondents and the value of each response option is calculated on the basis of their answers (for examples of such 'graded' multiple choice items, see Sample 2.5 below).

Sample 2.5. Multiple-choice attitude items from the 'Attitude/Motivation Test Battery' (Gardner, 1985, p. 181)

Scoring
Key

During French class, I would like:

2   (a) to have a combination of French and English spoken.
1   (b) to have as much English as possible spoken.
3   (c) to have only French spoken.

If there were a French Club in my school, I would:

2   (a) attend meetings once in a while.
3   (b) be most interested in joining.
1   (c) definitely not join.

2.4.3 Rank order items

It is a common human mental activity to rank order people, objects, or even abstract concepts, according to some criterion, and *rank order items* in questionnaires capitalize on our familiarity with this process. As the name suggests, these items contain some sort of a list and respondents are asked to order the items by assigning a number to them according to their preferences. Wilson and McClean (1994) warn us that it may be very demanding to arrange items in order of importance whenever there are more than five ranks requested, and it has also been found, more generally, that rank order items impose a more difficult task on the respondent than single-response items. Furthermore, unlike in a rating scale in which a person can assign the same value to several items (e.g., one can mark 'strongly agree' in all the items in a multi-item scale), in rank order items each sub-component must have a different value even though such a forced choice may not be natural in every case.

In my own research, I have tended to avoid rank order items because it is not easy to process them statistically. We cannot simply count the mean of the ranks for each item across the sample because the numerical values assigned to the items are not the same as in rating scales: they are only an easy technical method to indicate *order* rather than the *extent* of endorsement. That is, if something is ranked third, the value '3' does not necessarily mean that the degree of one's attitude is 3 out of, say, 5 (which would be the case in a Likert scale); it only means that the particular target's relevance/importance is, in the respondent's estimation, somewhere between the things ranked second and fourth; the actual value can be very near to the second and miles away from the forth or vice versa. To illustrate this, let us take a short list of items that we may need for travelling abroad:

- passport
- credit card
- tickets
- plumbing manual.

'Plumbing manual' would probably be ranked by everybody as the least necessary item in the list but by assigning a value of '4' or '1' to it (depending on which end we start counting from) its value would be only one less (or more) than the next one is the list, whereas in reality its value for travelling purposes is next to zero (unless you are a plumber...).

2.4.4 Numeric items

One item type that is seemingly open-ended but is, in effect, closed-ended can be labeled as a *numeric item*. These items ask for a specific numeric value, such as the respondent's age in years, or the number of foreign languages spoken by a person. What makes these items similar to closed questions is that we can anticipate the range of the possible answers and the respondent's task is to specify a particular value within the anticipated range. We could, in fact, list, for example for the 'age' item, all the possible numbers (e.g., between 5 and 100) for the respondent to choose from (in a multiple-choice fashion) but this would not be space-economical. However, computerized, on-line questionnaires often do provide these options in a pull-down menu for the respondent to click on the selected answer.

2.4.5 Checklists

Checklists are similar to rank order items in that they consist of a list of descriptive terms, attributes, or even objects, and respondents are instructed to mark the items on the list that apply to the particular question. For example, students might be asked to mark all the adjectives in a list of personality characteristics that describe their teacher. This evaluation would, then, yield a score for the teacher on each characteristic, indicating how many raters checked the particular adjective; that is, the person's score on each item can be set equal to the number of judges who checked it. In the teacher's case, a score of '0' on the 'fairness' item would mean that nobody thinks that the teacher is fair (which would be problematic). Because – unless otherwise instructed – different respondents may check a different number of items (e.g., someone may check almost all the adjectives, whereas another rater might check only one), this response set can have a pronounced effect on the scores and therefore some sort of grouping or statistical control is frequently used (Aiken, 1996).

2.5 OPEN-ENDED QUESTIONS

Open-ended questions include items where the actual question is not followed by response options for the respondent to choose from but rather by some blank space (e.g., dotted lines) for the respondent to fill. As we have seen in the previous chapter (in Section 1.3), questionnaires are not particularly suited for truly qualitative, exploratory research. Accordingly, they tend to have few open-ended questions and even the ones included are relatively short, with their 'openness' somehow restricted. Questionnaires are not the right place for essay questions.

In spite of this inherent limitation of the questionnaire as a research instrument (namely that due to the relatively short and superficial engagement of the respondents it cannot aim at more than obtaining a superficial, "thin" description of the target) open-ended questions still have merits. Although we cannot expect any soul-searching self-disclosure in the responses, by permitting greater freedom of expression, open-format items can provide a far greater "richness" than fully quantitative data. The open responses can offer graphic examples, illustrative quotes, and can also lead us to identify issues not previously anticipated. Furthermore, sometimes we need open-ended items for the simple reason that we do not know the range of possible answers and therefore cannot provide pre-prepared response categories. Oppenheim (1992) also points out that in some cases there may actually be good reasons for asking the same question both in an open and closed form.

The other side of the coin is that open-ended questions have certain serious disadvantages, most notably the following two:

- They take up precious 'respondent-availability time' and thus restrict the range of topics the questionnaire can contain.
- They are difficult to code in a reliable manner.

Because of these considerations, professional questionnaires tend not to include any real open-ended items; yet, my recommendation is that it might be worth experimenting with including some. Researchers agree that truly open questions (i.e., the ones that require quite a bit of writing) should be placed at the end rather than at the beginning of the questionnaire. In this way, they are not answered at the expense of the closed items: they do not discourage people from completing the questionnaire and do not prevent those who get bogged down with them from answering the other questions.

In my experience, open-ended questions work particularly well if they are not completely open but contain certain guidance. In the following we will look at four techniques to provide such guidance.

2.5.1 Specific open questions

Specific open questions ask about concrete pieces of information, such as facts about the respondent, past activities, or preferences (e.g., *Which is your favorite television program/weekend activity? What languages have you studied in the past?*). They can normally be answered in one line, which is usually explicitly marked on the questionnaire (e.g., with dots). The answers can sometimes be followed up with a 'Why?' question.

2.5.2 Clarification questions

Certain answers may be potentially so important that it is worth attaching a clarification question to them, for example in a 'routed' form:

```
If you rated the coursebook you are using as
"poor" or "very poor," please briefly explain
why. Write your answer here:

_____ _____

_____ _____
```

Clarification questions are also appropriate when there is an "Other" category in a multiple-choice item. Typically, "Please specify" is used and some space is left for the respondent to provide a statement.

2.5.3 Sentence completion items

A simple question is often less effective in eliciting a meaningful answer than an unfinished sentence beginning that the respondent needs to complete. I have successfully used this technique on various feedback forms in particular. A good completion item should be worded so that it directs the respondent's attention to a well-defined issue/area. Sometimes respondents are asked not to 'agonize' over the answers but jot down the first thing that comes to mind. For example:

```
One thing I liked about this activity is _____

_ _ _ _ _ _ _ _ _ _ _ _ _ _ _ _ _ _ _ _ _ _ _ _ _ _ _ _ _ _ _ _ _ _ _ _ _

One thing I didn't like about this activity is

_ _ _ _ _ _ _ _ _ _ _ _ _ _ _ _ _ _ _ _ _ _ _ _ _ _ _ _ _ _ _ _ _ _ _ _ _

I found this activity _ _ _ _ _ _ _ _ _ _ _ _ _ _ _ _ _ _ _ _

_ _ _ _ _ _ _ _ _ _ _ _ _ _ _ _ _ _ _ _ _ _ _ _ _ _ _ _ _ _ _ _ _ _ _ _ _
```

2.5.4 Short-answer questions

The term *'short-answer questions'* is sometimes used to distinguish these questions from 'essay questions' (which are not recommended in ordinary questionnaires and therefore will not be discussed). Short-answer questions involve a real exploratory enquiry about an issue;

that is, they require a more free-ranging and unpredictable response. As Gillham (2000, pp. 34-35) concludes, these questions:

> can be motivating for the respondent, and they enable the researcher to trawl for the unknown and the unexpected. One or two questions of this type can be a good way of finishing a questionnaire, which can otherwise easily leave respondents with the impression that their personal opinions or experiences have to fit the straitjacket of prescribed answers.

Gillham even recommends the inclusion of a completely open concluding question, such as, *"We have tried to make this questionnaire as comprehensive as possible but you may feel that there are things we have missed out. Please write what you think below, using an extra page if necessary"* (pp. 34-35).

Good short-answer questions are worded in such a focused way that the question can be answered succinctly, with a 'short answer' – this is usually more than a phrase and less than a paragraph (and certainly no more than two paragraphs). That is, short-answer questions do not ask about things in general, but deal with only one concept or idea. For example, rather than asking, *"What did you like about the workshop?"* it might be better to narrow down the question by asking, *"What was it you found most useful about the workshop?"*

One type of questionnaire that is almost always concluded by a few open-ended questions is college forms for students to evaluate their teachers/courses. A typical final sequence of questions is as follows: *What were the most effective aspects of this course? What were the least effective aspects of this course? How could this course be further improved?*

2.6 HOW TO WRITE GOOD ITEMS

Over the past 50 years, survey researchers have accumulated a considerable body of knowledge and experience about what makes a questionnaire item good and what the potential pitfalls are. However, most specialists also emphasize that question design is not a 100%

scientific activity because in order to write good items one also needs a certain amount of creativity and lots of common sense. Furthermore, alternative versions of questions must be rigorously piloted because in the absence of hard and fast theoretical rules, "tests of practicability must play a crucial role in questionnaire construction" (Moser & Kalton, 1971, p. 350)

Well said...

"The writing of successful attitude statements demands careful pilot work, experience, intuition and a certain amount of flair."

(Oppenheim, 1992, p. 180)

In the following I will summarize the do's and don'ts of item writing. Most of the material will concern the most common question types, rating scale items.

In writing questionnaire items...

"no amount of textbook admonition can take the place of common sense."

(Moser & Kalton, 1971, p. 310)

2.6.1 Drawing up an 'item pool'

It is generally recommended by survey specialists that when we get down to writing the actual items, we should start doing so without restricting ourselves to any number limitations. Let our imagination go free and create as many potential items as we can think of – this collection is referred to as the *item pool*. At this stage, successful item designers rely heavily on their own verbal creativity, but they also draw on two additional sources:

1. *Qualitative, exploratory data* gathered from informants, such as *notes* taken during talks and brainstorming in focus or discussion groups; recorded unstructured/semi-structured *interviews*; and *student essays* written around the subject of the enquiry. The best items are often the ones that sound as if they had been said by someone – so why not include phrases and sentences that have indeed been said by real informants?

2. *Borrowing questions* from established questionnaires. Questions that have been used frequently before must have been through extensive piloting and therefore the chances are that "most of the bugs will have been ironed out of them" (Sudman & Bradburn, 1983, p. 120). Of course, you will need to acknowledge the sources precisely.

Provided you acknowledge the sources...

"The best advice we can offer to those starting out to write attitude questions is to plagiarize. While plagiarism is regarded as a vice in most matters, it is a virtue in questionnaire writing – assuming, of course, that you plagiarize good quality questions."

(Sudman & Bradburn, 1983, p. 119)

2.6.2 Rules about item wording

Aim for short and simple items

Whenever possible, questionnaire items should be short, rarely exceeding 20 words. They should preferably be written in simple sentences rather than compound or complex sentences, and each should contain only one complete thought.

Quite so!

"… short questions are good questions."

(Brown, 2001, p. 45)

Use simple and natural language

As a rule, in questionnaire items we should always choose the simplest way to say something. Items need to be kept clear and direct, without any acronyms, abbreviations, colloquialisms, proverbs, jargon, or technical terms. We should try to speak the 'common language' and find synonyms for the "polysyllabic and Latinate constructions that come easily to the tongue of the college educated" (Converse & Presser, 1986, p. 10).

Oppenheim (1992) argues that the most important rule in writing rating scale statements is to make them *meaningful* and *interesting* to the respondents. As he points out, "There are many attitude scales which falter because the items have been composed in the office according to some theoretical plan and fail to arouse much interest in the respondents" (p. 179). The best items are the ones that sound like being taken from actual interviews, and Oppenheim encourages item writers not to refrain from using contentiously worded statements that include phrases relating to feelings, wishes, fears, and happiness.

Avoid ambiguous or loaded words and sentences

It goes without saying that any elements that might make the language of the items unclear or ambiguous need to be avoided. The most notorious of such elements are:

- Nonspecific adjectives or adverbs (e.g., good, easy, many, sometimes, often).

- Items containing universals such as 'all,' 'none,' 'never.'

- Modifying words such as 'only,' 'just,' 'merely' – these should be used with moderation.

- Words having more than one meaning.

- Loaded words (e.g., 'democratic,' 'modern,' 'natural,' 'free,' etc.), because they may elicit an emotional reaction that may bias the answer.

It is also obvious that loaded questions such as *"Isn't it reasonable to suppose that ...?"* or *"Don't you believe that...?"* are likely to bias the respondent toward giving a desired answer and should be rephrased in a neutral way.

Avoid negative constructions

Items that contain a negative construction (i.e., including 'no' or 'not') are deceptive because although they read OK, responding to them can be problematic. For example, what does a negative answer to a negative item mean? In order to avoid any possible difficulties, the best solution is to avoid the use of negatives altogether. In most cases negative items can be restated in a positive way by using verbs or adjectives that express the opposite meaning.

Avoid double-barreled questions

Double-barreled questions are those that ask two (or more) questions in one while expecting a single answer. For example, the question *"How are your parents?"* asks about one's mother and father, and cannot be answered simply if one of them is well and the other unwell. Indeed, questions dealing with pluralisms (children, students) often yield double-barreled questions, but compound questions also often fall into this category (e.g., *"Do you always write your homework and do it thoroughly?"*). With double-barreled questions even if respondents do provide an answer, there is no way of knowing which part of the question the answer concerned.

Avoid items that are likely to be answered the same way by everybody

In rating scales we should avoid statements that are likely to be endorsed by almost everyone or almost no one. In most cases these items are not informative and they are certainly difficult if not impossible to process statistically. Here is a recent example from my own research (Dörnyei & Clément, 2001): A questionnaire item asked students to rate the international role/importance of six countries, including the United States. As can be imagined, most respondents gave the U.S. the top score. However, as we found out in the analyses, this did not provide enough variance to compute certain statistical results involving this item, and in some cases – when in a particular subgroup (e.g., a school) every single person gave the top score – the computer treated the responses as missing data because of the total lack of variance.

Include both positively and negatively worded items

In order to avoid a response set in which the respondents mark only one side of a rating scale, it is worth including in the questionnaire both positively and negatively worded items. In addition, a balanced mixture might also reduce the harmful effects of the 'acquiescence bias' (cf. Section 1.2.2). The term 'negatively worded item' means that it focuses on negative rather than positive aspects of the target, and we should note that it is all too easy to fall into the trap of trying to express this negative aspect by using some sort of a negative construction (which has been previously warned against): I have found more than once in the past that even carefully designed and seemingly fine 'negatively worded items' had to be excluded from the questionnaire after a *post hoc* item analysis.

Ellard and Rogers' (1993, p. 17) "Ten Commandments of Question Writing"

I.   Thou shalt not create double-barreled items.

II.   Thou shalt not use 'no' and 'not' or words beginning with 'un.'

III. Thou shalt match the vocabulary used in items to the vocabulary of those who will respond to them.

IV.   Thou shalt not use complex grammatical forms.

V.   Thou shalt have 40% to 60% true- or agree-keyed items.

VI.   Thou shalt not use redundant or irrelevant items.

VII. Thou shalt not permit any loaded questions to appear in your questionnaire.

VIII. Thou shalt not mix response formats within a set of questions.

IX.   Thou shalt not permit a non-committal response.

X.   Thou shalt pretest questions before collecting data.

2.6.3 Writing sensitive items

If the previous section has (hopefully) suggested that item writing requires special attention to details, then this is even more so when writing *sensitive items*, that is, questions addressing issues that are not easy to talk about because they may ask about *confidential personal information, undesirable social behavior*, or information that might pose *potential threat* to the respondent.

Confidential personal information

With regard to questions that ask about *personal information* that is usually considered private, the best advice is that the fewer of them, the better. If they are really necessary for the survey then some sort of a justification and a renewed promise of confidentiality are in order (e.g., *"Finally, in order to help us to better interpret and classify your answers, would you mind telling us more about your personal and language learning background?"*).

Quite so!

"Classification questions … need a special introduction. After all, a respondent who agrees to answer questions about his leisure pursuits or to give his opinion about television may legitimately wonder why he should supply details about his family, his age, his education, his occupation, and even his income."

(Moser & Kalton, 1971, p. 316)

Undesirable social behavior

With regard to responses that might be felt will meet with *disapproval*, several strategies have been suggested in the literature. Wilson and McClean (1994) recommend that they can be diffused by the use of categories, or brands, for respondents to tick. In their seminal book on questionnaire design, Sudman and Bradburn (1983) devote a great deal of space to discussing sensitive items. Their practical suggestions to mitigate the undesirable nature of certain behaviors include:

- Wording the question in a way that it suggests that the behavior is rather common (e.g., *"Even the most conscientious teachers sometimes…"*).

- Assuming the occurrence of the behavior and asking about frequencies or other details rather than whether the behavior has occurred.

- Using authority to justify behavior (e.g., *"Many researchers now think…"*).

- Adopting a 'casual approach' (e.g., *"Did you happen to…?"*).

- Including reasons that explain the behavior (e.g., *"Does your busy schedule sometimes prevent you from…?"* or *"Have you had time to … recently?"*).

Aiken (1997) further suggests that by phrasing the question in a way that it refers to "other people" can encourage truthful responses, and the perceived importance of sensitive questions can also be reduced if they are embedded among other questions dealing with both sensitive and nonsensitive topics.

Potential threat

With regard to items in which an honest answer can pose some *real threat* to the respondent (e.g., questions about illegal activities, or asking students to evaluate their language teacher), the main task is to convince the respondents that their answers will remain confidential. Obviously, offering complete anonymity in such cases might be helpful, but this may not be feasible in certain complex research projects where we need to match the data with information obtained from other sources (cf. Section 2.1.3). In any case, additional gestures emphasizing confidentiality are always welcome. In a classroom study already mentioned (Clément et al., 1994) where a questionnaire was administered to class groups, we asked students to evaluate both the L2 teacher and the course, and applied three confidence-building strategies:

• The questionnaire administrator was a representative of the university and thus external to the school – a fact that was sufficiently emphasized.

• We handed out envelopes in which students put their completed questionnaires and which they then sealed.

• The questionnaire administrator went around the classroom and stamped the envelopes with a university stamp on the seals.

Some questions can pose a threat not only to the respondent but also to the people or institutions the questionnaire is about. For example, few teachers are likely to be happy to allow the administration of a questionnaire in their classes that explicitly asks the students to evaluate the quality of their teaching. Interestingly, Gardner and Smythe (1981) report that educational institutions found semantic differential scales (cf. Section 2.4) less objectionable than complete evaluative statements when talking about such sensitive issues. It seems that the fact that these items do not spell out the issues in detail but only provide pairs of bipolar adjectives make them less offensive.

2.7 GROUPING AND ORDERING ITEMS

Once all the items to be included in the questionnaire have been written or collected, we need to decide on their order. Item sequence is a significant factor because the context of a question can have an impact on its interpretation and the response given to it. Indeed, the meaning of almost any question can be altered by the adjacent questions. However, it is usually acknowledged that research has not as yet generated any specific theoretical rules to order questions, beyond some broad suggestions (Robson, 1993). Let us have a look at the four main ordering principles.

Clear and orderly structure

The most important aspect of sequencing questions is to ensure that the respondents' overall impression is that the structure is well-organized and orderly. If the ordering of questions is unpredictable or seemingly haphazard, it will frustrate respondents and make the study appear ill-considered and amateurish (Newell, 1993). Neither the content nor the style of the questionnaire should "jump around" (Aiken, 1997) – the items should seem as a series of logically organized sequences. To achieve this, we need to follow certain organizing principles.

One organizing principle should be the *item format*. If the questionnaire contains items of different types, these need to be clustered together into well marked sub-sections, separated from each other by a clear set of instructions to highlight the format change for the respondent. Similarly, questions that deal with the same *topic* should be grouped together. In order to make the progression from topic to topic smoother, we may include short linking sentences such as, *"In this section we'll move on to look at more specific aspects of...".* Content-based organization, however, does not mean that the items in a multi-item scale (cf. Section 2.3.2) should be next to each other – the repetitive content may frustrate the respondents. What I usually do is take 4-5 content areas that are related to each other and then mix up the constituent items randomly.

Opening questions

Just like with any other piece of writing, the initial section of a questionnaire is particularly important in that it sets the tone. This is partly the reason that instructions (cf. Sections 2.2.2 and 3.3.7) play a significant role, and this is also why the first few 'opening' questions should be carefully selected. In order to create a pleasant first impression, the starter questions need to be interesting, relatively simple yet at the same time focused on some important and salient aspect, and certainly non-threatening/sensitive.

Factual (or 'personal' or 'classification') questions at the end

As Oppenheim (1992) concludes, novice researchers typically start to design a questionnaire by putting a rather forbidding set of questions at the top of a blank sheet of paper, asking for name, address, marital status, number of children, religion, and so on. These personal/classification questions tend to be very off-putting: Having been through the various introductory phases, respondents are now ready to look at some interesting questions dealing with the topic of the study. Instead, they are faced with a set of 'personal' questions not unlike those contained in the many bureaucratic forms we have to fill in when, for example, applying for a passport or registering in a hotel. This can result in a kind of anticlimax in the respondents and it may be difficult to rekindle their enthusiasm again. Thus, such personal questions are best left at the end of the questionnaire.

There is also a second reason why factual questions should not be introduced too early, and this concerns their sensitive nature. As discussed in Section 2.1.3, in many cultures issues like age, level of education, or marital status are personal and private matters, and if we ask them near the beginning of the questionnaire they might create some resistance in the respondents (*"What business of yours is this...?"*), or, in cases where respondents are asked to provide their name, this might remind them of the non-anonymous nature of the survey, which in turn may inhibit some of their answers.

Open-ended questions at the end

As discussed in Section 2.5, if we include real open-ended questions that require substantial and creative writing, it is preferable to place them near the end rather than at the beginning of the questionnaire. In this way, their potential negative consequences (e.g., the required work can put some people off; others might get bogged down and spend most of the available time and mental energy agonizing over what they should write) will not affect the previous items. In addition, some people find it psychologically more acceptable to put in the necessary work if they have already invested in the questionnaire and if they know that this is the final task.

2.8 COMPUTER PROGRAMS FOR CONSTRUCTING QUESTIONNAIRES

Because market research – a booming business area – utilizes questionnaires for various types of surveys, several software companies have developed commercial computer programs to cater to these needs: Currently there are over 30 available desktop packages that combine questionnaire design, data collection, and data analysis. However, as Macer (1999) summarizes, few packages rise to the challenge of each stage in the process with the same degree of accomplishment, and development effort often tends to gravitate to some areas at the expense of others. For comprehensive listings and descriptions of the programs on the market, see for example the Research Software Central database (http://www.macer.co.uk/rscentral/rscentral.html) or the database of the Association for Survey Computing (U.K.), which contains a classified listing of 123 software packages related to survey research, with attributes and suppliers (http://www.asc.org.uk/Register/index.htm).

Here I will introduce one computer program that I am familiar with: *SphinxSurvey*, distributed by Scolari/Sage (the publishers of such well-known qualitative data analysis software as NUD*IST and NVivo), is an integrated, PC-based Windows package for conducting questionnaire-based surveys (for a review, see Macer, 1999). It has built-in functions to help the user to design and print professional questionnaires with ease. The program can handle a variety of question types, including open and closed questions. Similar questions can be grouped and conditional jumps can be defined to permit complex question routings (e.g., if people answer 'yes' to Question X, they should move to Question Y). In addition, extensive question libraries can be developed and used to aid the preparation of an item pool.

SphinxSurvey is certainly a useful tool in providing a computerized framework for quick and professional questionnaire construction (the data processing functions of the program will be analyzed in Section 4.5). The novice researcher will find various ready-made options to choose from by simply clicking on items in the menu. The display format is quite flexible and the final result is fairly attractive. Because of the paramount importance of the appropriate layout (cf. Section 2.1.2), I would still design the final version of a questionnaire on a more powerful word processor, but in many situations the available formats are sufficient.

2.9 PILOTING THE QUESTIONNAIRE AND CONDUCTING ITEM ANALYSIS

Because in questionnaires so much depends on the actual wording of the items (even minor differences can change the response pattern) an integral part of questionnaire construction is 'field testing,' that is, *piloting* the questionnaire at various stages of its development on a sample of people who are similar to the target sample the instrument has been designed for. These trial runs allow the researcher to collect feedback about how the instrument works and whether it performs the job it has been designed for. Based on this information, we can make alterations and fine-tune the final version of the questionnaire.

Well...

"if you do not have the resources to pilot-test your questionnaire, don't do the study."

(Sudman & Bradburn, 1983, p. 283)

The pilot test can highlight questions:

- whose wording may be ambiguous;
- which are too difficult for the respondent to reply to;
- which may, or should be, eliminated because, contrary to the initial expectations, they do not provide any unique information or because they turn out to measure something irrelevant;
- which – in the case of open-ended questions – are problematic to code into a small set of meaningful categories.

Piloting can also indicate problems or potential pitfalls concerning:

- the administration of the questionnaire;
- the scoring and processing of the answers.

Valuable feedback can also be gained about:

- the overall appearance of the questionnaire;
- the clarity of the instructions;
- the appropriateness of the cover letter (if there is one);
- the length of time necessary to complete the instrument.

Finally, this is also the phase when omissions in the coverage of content can be identified.

The importance of the piloting is in sharp contrast with the reality that so many researchers completely omit the pilot stage from their research design. Although this is understandable from a personal point of view because researchers at this stage are eager to get down to the survey and see the results, from a measurement perspective this practice is untenable. Regardless of how experienced the questionnaire designer is, any attempt to shortcut the piloting stage will seriously jeopardize the psychometric quality of the questionnaire (Moser & Kalton, 1971). Furthermore, my experience is that by patiently going through the careful editing procedures we can avoid a great deal of frustration and possible extra work later on.

Sometimes the omission of the pilot stage is not due to the lack of will/interest but rather to insufficient time. To do it well, piloting takes up a substantial period, which has often not been included in the timing of the research design. As we will see below, piloting is a stepwise process that, when properly done, can take several weeks to complete. This is usually much more than was originally intended for this phase of the research.

Absolutely!

"Questionnaires do not emerge fully-fledged; they have to be created or adapted, fashioned and developed to maturity after many abortive test flights. In fact, every aspect of a survey has to be tried out beforehand to make sure that it works as intended."

(Oppenheim, 1992, p. 47)

So when and what shall we pilot? While it is useful to have 'ongoing piloting' by continuously discussing every aspect of questionnaire design with a colleague or a friend, there are two points where a more formal trial run is needed: (1) Once the item pool has been com-

pleted, and (2) when a complete, almost final version of the questionnaire has been prepared.

2.9.1 Initial piloting of the item pool

The first time in the questionnaire construction process that some external feedback is indispensable is when we have prepared an initial
item pool (cf. Section 2.6.1), that is, a large list of possible items, and
we are ready to reduce the number of questions to the intended final
number. The initial piloting of the item pool usually consists of the
following steps:

- Select three or four people who are motivated to spend some time
  to help you and whose opinion you value. Some of them should
  not be specialists in the field – they are very useful in locating unnecessary jargon; others may be people who are accustomed to
  survey research or who know the target population well. In any
  case, as Converse and Presser (1986) so realistically state, at this
  stage we are likely to end up with "that familiar source of forced
  labor – colleagues, friends, and family" (p. 53).

- Ask them to go through the items and answer them, and then to
  provide feedback about their reactions and the answers they have
  given. The best method to conduct this phase is for you to be present while they are working: this way you can observe their
  reactions (e.g., hesitations or uncertainties) and can note and respond to any spontaneous questions or comments.

- Once they have gone through all the items, you may ask for any
  general comments and can initiate a brainstorming session.

It may be useful to provide your pilot group with some basic
guidelines to focus on. These can include the following:

- They should mark any items whose wording they don't like; if
  they can suggest an improvement, so much the better!

- They should mark any items whose meaning is not 100 percent clear; again, suggestions are welcome.

- They should mark any items that they consider unnecessary.

- They should try and think of anything else that might be worth asking about.

Very important!

"you may find that you have put so much personal time and effort into developing the questionnaire that it becomes 'your baby.' If someone is subsequently critical of it, you may find yourself reacting as if you have been personally attacked. Perhaps, rule number one in the critiquing/revision process is that the creator should never take the criticism personally."

(Brown, 2001, p. 62)

2.9.2 Final piloting ('dress rehearsal')

Based on the feedback received from the initial pilot group we can normally put together a near-final version of the questionnaire that 'feels' OK and that does not have any obvious glitches. However, we still do not know how the items will work in actual practice, that is, whether the selected respondents will reply to the items in the manner intended by the questionnaire designers. There is only one way to find out: by administering the questionnaire to a group of respondents who are in every way similar to the target population the instrument was designed for. This is usually an 'undeclared' pretest whereby the respondents are not told that this is a questionnaire under construction. (Converse & Presser, 1986)

How big should this final pilot group be? It need not be very large; the typical sample size at this stage is around 50 (+/- 20). This number will already allow the researcher to conduct some meaningful item analysis, which is the next, and final, step in the questionnaire construction process. In addition, if the final piloting phase did not result in major changes, it may be possible to use at least some of the obtained data for the purpose of the 'real' investigation.

2.9.3 Item analysis

Item analysis can be conducted at two different points in the survey process:

- After the final piloting stage – in this case the results are used to fine-tune and finalize the questionnaire.

- After the administration of the final questionnaire – after such a *'post hoc analysis'* the results are used to screen out any items that have not worked properly.

The procedures in both cases are similar. They usually involve checking three aspects of the response pattern:

(1) *Missing responses* and possible signs that the instructions were not understood correctly. If some items are left out by several respondents, that should serve as an indication that something is not right: Perhaps the item is too difficult, too ambiguous, or too sensitive; or perhaps its location in the questionnaire is such that it is easy to be overlooked. Also, a careful visual examination of the completed questionnaire might reveal some further response irregularities, for example in the way respondents marked their answers.

(2) The *range of the responses* elicited by each item. It was argued in Section 2.6.2 that we should avoid including items that are endorsed by almost everyone or by almost no one because they are

difficult if not impossible to process statistically (since statistical procedures require a certain amount of variation in the scores). Although, as Brown (2001) remarks, the lack of variation may well be the true state of affairs in the group, it may be useful in many cases to increase item variation by adding additional response categories or rewording the question.

(3) The *internal consistency* of multi-item scales. The gist of Section 2.3.2 was that – for the sake of reducing the unpredictable impact of item wording – questionnaires should contain multi-item scales, rather than single items, to focus on any particular content domain. It is obvious, however, that multi-item scales are only effective if the items within a scale work together in a homogeneous manner, that is, if they measure the same target area. In psychometric terms this means that each item on a scale should correlate with the other items and with the total scale score, which has been referred to as Likert's criterion of 'Internal Consistency' (Anderson, 1985). Following this principle, a simple way of selecting items for a scale is to compute correlation coefficients for each potential item with the total scale score and to retain the items with the highest correlations. There are also other, more sophisticated statistical methods to check and improve internal consistency – these will be summarized in Section 4.3.5.

3

Administering the Questionnaire

One area in which a questionnaire study can go very wrong concerns the procedures used to *administer* the questionnaire. Strangely enough, this aspect of survey research has hardly ever been discussed in the L2 literature – questionnaire administration is often considered a mere technical issue relegated to the discretion of the research assistants. This is wrong; there is ample evidence in the measurement literature that questionnaire administration procedures play a significant role in affecting the quality of the elicited responses. In this chapter, I will first look at the selection of an appropriate *sample*, then discuss the various *types* of questionnaire administration and the *strategies* that can be employed to promote positive questionnaire attitudes and involvement on the part of the respondents. Finally, I will address the issue of *confidentiality/anonymity* and other *ethical responsibilities* survey researchers have.

3.1 SELECTING THE SAMPLE

The most frequent question asked by novice researchers who are planning to use questionnaires in their investigation is *"How many people do I need to survey?"* In measurement terms this question can be formulated as *"How large should my sample be?"* And a second question to follow is, *"What sort of people shall I select?,"* or in other words, *"Who shall my sample consist of?"* Let us start answering these key questions with the latter pair.

3.1.1 Sampling procedures

Broadly speaking, the *sample* is the group of people whom researchers actually examine and the *population* is the group of people whom the survey is about. For example, the population in a study might be EFL learners in Taiwanese secondary schools and the actual sample might involve three Taiwanese secondary classes. That is, the target population of a study consists of all the people to whom the survey's findings are to be applied or generalized.

Why don't we include every member of the population in the survey? This is a valid question and, indeed, there is one particular survey type where we do just that: the 'census.' In most other cases, however, investigating the whole population is not necessary and would in fact be a waste of resources. By adopting appropriate *sampling procedures* to select a smaller number of people to be questioned we can save a considerable amount of time, cost, and effort and can still come up with accurate results – opinion polls, for example, succeed in providing national projections based on as few as 1,000–3,000 respondents. The key question, then, is what do we mean by 'appropriate sampling procedures?'

A good sample is very similar to the target population in its most important general characteristics (e.g., age, gender, ethnicity, educational background, academic capability, social class, or socioeconomic status, etc.) and in all the more specific features that are known to be significantly related to the items included on the questionnaire (e.g., L2 learning background or the amount and type of L2 instruction received). That is, the sample is a subset of the population which is *representative* of the whole population. Sampling procedures have been designed to ensure this representativeness.

Selecting a truly representative sample is a painstaking and costly process, and several highly technical monographs have been written about the topic (e.g., Cochran, 1977; Levy & Lemeshow, 1999). In most L2 survey research it is unrealistic or simply not feasible to aim for perfect representativeness in the psychometric sense. Therefore, in the following overview I will not discuss the details of the statistical procedures of 'probability sampling,' which is the generic term used for a number of scientific procedures such as simple random sampling, systematic sampling, stratified random sampling, and cluster sampling.

Convenience or opportunity sampling

The most common sample type in L2 research is a *convenience* or *opportunity sample*, where an important criterion of sample selection is the convenience for the researcher: Members of the target population will be selected for the purpose of the study if they meet certain practical criteria, such as geographical proximity, availability at a certain time, or easy accessibility. If we decide, for example, to study a class group because we have good contacts with the particular school, that would be a case of convenience sampling. Convenience samples are usually *'purposive,'* which means that besides the relative ease of accessibility, participants also have to possess certain key characteristics that are related to the purpose of the investigation (Aiken, 1997).

Snowball sampling

Snowball sampling involves a 'chain reaction' whereby the researcher identifies a few people who meet the criteria of the particular study and then asks these participants to identify further members of the population. This technique is useful when studying groups whose membership is not readily identifiable (e.g., teenage gang members); an example in L2 research would be asking learners with extreme L2 use anxiety to name/recruit other highly anxious peers they know.

Quota sampling

In *quota sampling* the researcher defines certain distinct subgroups (e.g., boys and girls, or age cohorts) and determines the proportion of the population that belongs to each of these subgroups (e.g., when targeting language teachers, determining that the female-male ratio among them is 70%-30% in a particular setting). The actual sample, then, is selected in a way as to reflect these proportions (i.e. 70% of the sample will be women). In fact, the common intention to select a roughly equal number of boys and girls for the sample is in accordance with the spirit of quota sampling (provided, of course, that this ratio is true of the particular target population). Thus, quota sampling is a way of controlling various relevant population characteristics.

Random sampling

The key component of scientific sampling procedures is *random sampling*. This involves selecting members of the population to be included in your sample on a completely random basis, a bit like drawing numbers from a hat (e.g., by numbering each member and then asking the computer to generate random numbers). The assumption underlying this procedure is that it minimizes the effects of any extraneous or subjective variables that might affect the outcome of the survey study. Combining random sampling with some form of rational grouping is a particularly effective method for surveys with a specific focus (Aiken, 1997). In *area sampling* or *cluster sampling* or *stratified random sampling* the population is divided into groups, or 'strata,' and a random sample of a proportionate size is selected from each group. In studies following this method, the population is usually stratified on more than one variable and samples are selected at random from the groups defined by the intersections of the various strata (e.g., we would sample female learners of Spanish, aged 13-14, who attend a particular type of instructional program in a particular location).

3.1.2 How large should the sample be?

When researchers ask the question, *"How large should the sample be?"* what they usually mean is *"How small a sample can I get away with?"* Therefore, the often quoted 'the larger, the better' principle is singularly unhelpful for them. Unfortunately, there are no hard and fast rules in setting the optimal sample size; the final answer to the 'how large/small?' question should be the outcome of the researcher considering several broad guidelines:

(1) In the survey research literature a range of between 1%-10% of the population is usually mentioned as the 'magic sampling fraction,' depending on how careful the selection has been (i.e., the more scientific the sampling procedures applied, the smaller the sample size can be, which is why opinion polls can produce accurate predictions from samples as small as 0.1% of the population).

(2) From a purely statistical point of view, a basic requirement is that the sample should have a *normal distribution*, and a rule of thumb to achieve this, offered by Hatch and Lazaraton (1991), is that the sample should include 30 or more people. However, Hatch and Lazaraton also emphasize that this is not an absolute rule, because smaller sample sizes can be compensated for by using certain special statistical procedures.

(3) From the perspective of *statistical significance* (cf. Section 4.3.6), the principal concern is to sample enough learners for the expected results to be able to reach statistical significance. Because in L2 studies meaningful correlations reported in journal articles have often been as low as 0.30 and 0.40, a good rule of thumb is that we need around 50 participants to make sure that these coefficients are significant and we do not lose potentially important results. However, certain multivariate statistical procedures require more than 50 participants; for factor analysis, for example, we need a minimum of 100 but preferably more subjects.

(4) A further important consideration is whether there are any distinct subgroups within the sample which may be expected to behave differently from the others. If we can identify such subgroups in advance (e.g., in most L2 studies of school children, girls have been found to perform differently from boys), we should set the sample size so that the minimum size applies to the *smallest subgroup* to allow for effective statistical procedures.

(5) When setting the final sample size, it is advisable to leave a decent *margin* to provide for unforeseen or unplanned circumstances. For example, some participants are likely to drop out of at least some phases of the project; some questionnaires will always

have to be disqualified for one reason or another; and – in relation to Point 4 above – we may also detect unexpected subgroups that need to be treated separately.

3.1.3 The problem of respondent self-selection

To conclude the discussion of the various sampling issues for research purposes in general, we need to highlight a potential pitfall that might put the validity of the survey at risk: the *problem of participant self-selection*. This refers to cases when for various reasons the actual composition of the sample is not only the function of some systematic selection process but also of factors related to the respondents' own willingness to participate. Problems can arise, for example, when:

- researchers invite *volunteers* to take part in a study (occasionally even offering money to compensate for the time spent);

- the design allows for a high degree of *dropout* (or 'mortality'), in which case participants self-select themselves *out* of the sample;

- participants are free to choose whether they fill in the questionnaire or not (e.g., in *postal surveys*).

Self-selection is inevitable to some extent because few questionnaire surveys can be made compulsory; however, in some cases – e.g., in the examples above – it can reach such a degree that there is a good chance that the resulting sample will not be similar to the population. For example, volunteers may be different from non-volunteers in their aptitude, motivation, or some other basic characteristic, and dropouts also may share some common features that will be underrepresented in the sample with their departure (e.g., dropouts may be more unmotivated than their peers and therefore their departure might make the remaining participants' general level of motivation unnaturally high). Consequently, the sample may lose its representative character, which of course would prevent any meaningful generalizability.

Quite so!

"The problem is that the types of respondents who return questionnaires may be a specific type of 'eager-beaver' or 'gung-ho' respondent. Thus the results of the survey can only be generalized to 'eager-beaver' or 'gung-ho' people in the population rather than to the entire population."

(Brown, 2001, p. 85)

The scope of the self-selection problem can be illustrated by the fact that 'impersonal' questionnaires (e.g., mail surveys) typically attract an initial response rate of only around 30%, and over 50% can already be seen as a good response (Gillham, 2000). Although there are several ways of increasing respondent motivation and subsequent return rate (cf. Sections 3.2.1 and 3.3), with the exception of 'captive groups' (e.g., students surveyed in a lecture hall as part of some scheduled instructional activity), we can always expect a considerable self-selection effect, which suggests that – given that in order to ensure sample representativeness, a response rate of at least 80% is considered necessary – survey samples are frequently biased in some unknown manner (Aiken, 1997).

3.2 MAIN TYPES OF QUESTIONNAIRE ADMINISTRATION

In social research the most common form of administering questionnaires is *by mail*. Educational research is different in this respect because administration *by hand* is just as significant (if not more) as postal surveys. Within non-postal surveys, we can distinguish two distinct subtypes, one-to-one administration and group administration. Because the administration method has a significant bearing on the format and to some extent also on the content of the questionnaire, we need to examine separately the special features of the different types of questionnaire administration.

3.2.1 Administration by mail

The unique characteristic of *postal administration* is that the researcher has no contact with the respondent except for a cover letter he/she has written to accompany the questionnaire. In addition, mailed questionnaires are often in competition for the addressee's attention with various sorts of circulars, catalogues, and junk mail also received through mail, and the two factors together largely explain why the return rate of such surveys is often well below 30%. Such a low return rate, of course, undermines the reliability of the sample (cf. Section 3.1.3) and therefore if we decide to conduct a survey by mail we need to adopt a number of special strategies that have been found to increase the respondents' willingness to complete and return the questionnaire.

The cover letter

In the absence of a 'live' contact person, the *cover letter* has the difficult job to 'sell' the survey, that is, to create rapport with the respondents and to convince them about the importance of the survey and of their role in contributing to it. In addition to this public relations function, the cover letter also needs to provide certain specific information and directions. To write a letter that meets all these requirements is not easy, particularly in view of the fact that it needs to be *short* at the same time. If it is more than a page it is likely to be tossed aside and then find its way into the trashcan unread. So writing this letter is something we do not want to rush.

Cover letters usually address the following points:

- Who the writer is.
- The organization that is sponsoring or conducting the study.

- What the survey is about and why this is important or socially useful.
- Why the recipient's opinion is important and how he/she was selected.
- Assurance that all responses will be kept confidential.
- How to return the completed questionnaire.
- The date by which the completed questionnaire should be returned.
- What to do if questions arise (e.g., a contact name and telephone number).
- Possible reward for participation.
- Thank you!
- Signature, preferably by a person of recognized stature.
- Attached stamped addressed envelope.

Gillham (2000) warns us that even though the questionnaire is sent out together with the cover letter, the two often get separated. Therefore, it is important that the questionnaire itself be self-contained and also include vital pieces of information such as the return address and the date of return (which, in my experience, should be around 10 days after receiving the questionnaire).

Follow-up letters

After you have posted the questionnaires, an anxious period of waiting begins. Based on his experience, Gillham (2000) provides a rule-of-thumb estimate that the response you have received by the end of 10 days will be about half of what you can expect to get back in the long run. In order to receive the other half, you need to send a follow-up letter (about 2½ to 3 weeks after the original mailing). This second mailing is well worth the effort as it can increase the response rate by as much as 30%. With regard to the content of this letter, Gillham makes the following suggestions:

- We need not be too apologetic.

- We should reiterate the importance of the study and of the *participants' contribution.*

- There is no need to talk about the response rate to date.

- We should enclose a further copy of the questionnaire and another stamped addressed envelope "in case they did not receive or have mislaid the original one" (p. 48).

In another ten days' time a second follow-up letter can be sent.

Guidelines for increasing mail survey return rates

How can we increase the willingness of the recipients to take the time and trouble to complete and return the postal survey? The strategies most frequently mentioned in the measurement literature are as follows (see also Section 3.3, which offers general – i.e., not restricted to postal surveys in particular – strategies to promote respondent attitudes):

- *Pre-survey letters* give advance notice about the purpose and nature of the forthcoming questionnaire and can create a favorable climate for the survey.

- *Careful timing of the mailing.* First, it is advisable to avoid mailings at holiday periods or particularly busy times of the year. Second, questionnaires that arrive in the second half of the week are more likely to be dealt with over the weekend.

- Make the opening and concluding questions in the questionnaire particularly *interesting:* the former to whet the respondents' appetite and the latter to encourage the return of the questionnaire.

- Emphasize that the recipient's responses are *needed* and *valuable.*

- The reputation of a prestigious *sponsoring organization* may be the necessary final push for the recipient to get down to completing the questionnaire. If some of the questions are related to the respondent's workplace, it is important that the organization in charge of the survey is seen as independent.

- With postal surveys, making the *layout* of the questionnaire (cf. Section 2.1.2) attractive is more important than with hand-delivered questionnaires.

- Use good quality *paper* and *envelope*.

- The *address* should be typed and special care needs to be taken that the person's name is spelled correctly and that the person's title is accurate – writing 'Miss' instead of 'Mrs.' is seen as annoying by some and others do not like the title 'Ms.' Susan Gass (personal communication, 18 January, 2002) has successfully used a 'stopgap' strategy in the past in cases in which she was not sure about the exact title by only writing 'M.' She found that this is less disturbing for people with strong feelings about either Ms. or Miss than using the wrong title.

- Send the questionnaire by *first-class mail* or some equivalent in order to emphasize that it is not one of those 'bulk deliveries.'

- Send a small *token of appreciation* as it might be helpful because it evokes the human instinct of reciprocation.

Unfortunately, even if we observe all these guidelines we cannot expect high respondent motivation. A return rate of more than 50 percent can be considered satisfactory and response rates higher than 80 percent are rarely obtained (Aiken, 1997).

Regrettably...

"An unexpectedly poor response to questionnaires can be a salutary experience for the novice researcher."

(Gillham, 2000, p. 9)

3.2.2 One-to-one administration

One-to-one administration refers to a situation when someone delivers the questionnaire by hand to the designated person and arranges the completed form to be picked up later (e.g., handing out questionnaires to colleagues at work). This is a much more personal form of administration than mail surveys and therefore the chances for the questionnaires to be returned are significantly better. The personal contact also allows the questionnaire administrator to create rapport with the respondent, to explain the purpose of the enquiry, and to encourage cooperation. Furthermore, with young children (i.e., less than ten years old) the administrator can be present while they complete the questionnaire to be available if help is needed.

Oppenheim (1992) draws attention to a potential pitfall of one-to-one administration: When such a questionnaire administration strategy is adopted, researchers often utilize the help of someone in an official capacity on site who is not a skilled interviewer (e.g., a teacher or a manager or some other contact person in a targeted institution). However, there is a danger that without appropriate briefing such persons may, with the best intentions, introduce fatal biases. The face-to-face survey administrator needs to cover all the points that the cover letter does in postal surveys (cf. Section 3.2.1) and yet, when we ask mediators to hand out a few questionnaires in the contexts they move around in, how often do we train them properly for doing this job properly? When it comes to *group administration* (cf. Section 3.2.3) researchers typically place more emphasis on standardizing the administration procedures and with postal surveys a carefully composed cover letter can do the job; however, one-to-one administration somehow slips into the gap between the two and it is often assumed that exercising the 'personal touch' with the respondents (which is the mediator's forte) can substitute for professional administration procedures. A possible remedy is to give the administrator a *cue card* with the main points to be covered briefly when handing out each questionnaire.

3.2.3 Group administration

In L2 research, *group administration* is the most common method of having questionnaires completed. One reason for this is that the typical targets of the surveys are language learners studying within institutional contexts, and it is often possible to arrange to administer the instrument to them while they are assembled together, for example, as part of a lesson or slotted between certain other organized activities. The other reason for the popularity of this administration format is that it can overcome some of the problems just mentioned with regard to postal surveys or one-to-one administration. Groups of students are typically 'captive groups' in the sense that a response rate of nearly 100% can be achieved with them, and because a few questionnaire administrators can collect a very large number of questionnaires, it is easier to make sure that all of them are adequately trained for the job.

Group administration is the format I have used most in my past research and it is my overall experience that as long as the questionnaire is well designed and the administration situation well prepared in advance, very good results can be achieved. There are, however, some important points to consider:

- Because respondents have to work individually, Oppenheim (1992) reports that this format may not be appropriate for children under about age 10.

- With larger groups, or with groups of less mature kids, more than one field worker at a time is needed to help to answer questions and to distribute/collect the questionnaires.

- Oppenheim (1992) also warns us that in group administration 'contamination' through copying, talking, or asking questions is a constant danger.

- The negative influence of deviant kids may create an inappropriate climate for sincere and thoughtful work.

3.3 STRATEGIES TO INCREASE THE QUALITY AND QUANTITY OF PARTICIPANT RESPONSE

The main message of this section can be summarized in three words: *Administration procedures matter!* It was emphasized more than once in the previous two chapters that the 'Achilles heel' of questionnaires as measuring instruments is that it is difficult to get respondents to spend enough time and effort completing them. Educational researchers are in a slightly better position in this respect because school children are often willing to work hard on a task simply because it is assigned to them, but the older the students get the less this is so. Adults – and young adults – are usually perfectly aware of the fact that they have nothing to gain from participating in the survey and may also see the questionnaire as an intrusion both literally and meta-phorically. Haven't we all thought at one time or another that a questionnaire we have received was nothing but a nuisance? As Gillham (2000, p. 10) rightly notes, "the market is questionnaire saturated," and even if someone completes and returns a questionnaire, the chances are that he/she will not have worked hard at the answers.

Regrettably...

"People tend not to take questionnaires seriously; their answers may be frankly frivolous."

(Gillham, 2000, p. 13)

In view of these handicaps, the researcher's task to motivate the respondents to give truthful and thoughtful answers to all the relevant items on the questionnaire might seem daunting if not impossible. The good news, however, is that people in general like to express their opinions and do not mind answering questions as long as they think that the survey is related to a worthy cause and that their opinion matters. Thus, if we take sufficient care planning and executing the administration process, we can successfully build on these human characteristics and can secure the cooperation of our informants. The following strategies have been found effective in achieving this objective.

3.3.1 Advance notice

Surprising as it may sound, the administration of the questionnaire really does not start when the survey administrator first appears on the scene with a bundle of sheets in his/her hand. In most cases several important things about the survey have been determined in the respondent by that time. For example, Sudman and Bradburn (1983) conclude that most refusals to cooperate occur before the interviewers have had a chance to explain fully the purposes of the survey. In a paper entirely devoted to analyzing test/questionnaire administration, Clemans (1971, p. 193) also emphasizes that "To a very considerable extent, the examinee's attitudes toward the test will have been formed before the day it is administered."

One important factor that influences the respondent's initial disposition is the person's general attitude toward questionnaires. Some people simply cannot stand any kinds of self-completed forms and there isn't much we can do about it. What we *can* do, however, is to announce the questionnaire a few days in advance and to send each participant a printed leaflet that explains the purpose and nature of the questionnaire, contains a few sample items, and invites participation. This is an effective method of generating a positive climate for the administration and it also reduces the anxiety caused by the unexpected and unknown. Such advance notice also raises the 'professional' feel of the survey, which in turn promotes positive participant attitudes.

3.3.2 Attitudes conveyed by teachers, parents, and other authority figures

Data gathering often takes place in someone's 'home ground.' In school settings, for example, students usually hear about the survey first from their teachers. The important thing to note with respect to this is that participants are rather quick to pick up their superiors' (e.g., teachers' or bosses') attitude toward the survey and only acquiesce if the message they receive is positive. Similarly, parental disposition can also have a major impact on students' willingness to respond. It is therefore an imperative to *win the support* of all these authority figures in advance.

An important aspect of securing the cooperation of the people who are in charge within the questionnaire administration context is to start at the top. Even if we have personal contacts in a particular school, it is advisable to approach the head teacher (or even the chief education officer of the region) first and ask for a formal consent to approach the designated teachers to discuss the possibility of conducting research among their pupils. The official request, which is usually a formal letter, should obviously outline the aims, the design, and the methods of the research, and should offer some rationale in terms of the survey's relevance to education (Oppenheim, 1992)

3.3.3 Respectable sponsorship

A further factor that might work positively for survey administrators before they have even opened their mouths is some respectable and impressive *institutional sponsorship* of the study. If we can claim to represent an organization that is esteemed highly by the respondents, the positive reputation is likely to be projected onto the survey. If our institution is less known among the participants, a short leaflet describing its main features (and its strengths!) might tip the balance in favor of the survey. Similarly, a letter of introduction from someone influential can also boost questionnaire attitudes.

3.3.4 The behavior of the survey administrator

After all the preliminary considerations, we have finally arrived at the actual day of the survey. The survey administrator is facing the participants (obviously, this section does not apply to postal surveys) and is ready to launch into his/her pep talk. However, in line with the saying, 'Actions speak louder than words,' we need to be aware that our behavior is also conveying important messages to the respondents. The administrators of the questionnaire are, in many ways, identified with the whole survey and, therefore, everything about them matters:

- *clothes* should be business-like but certainly not more formal than what is typical in the given environment;

- the way they *introduce themselves* is important: friendliness is imperative and smiling usually breaks the ice effectively;

- *overall conduct* should be professional to represent the serious character of the survey without being stiff and unnatural.

A crucial aspect of the survey administrators' behavior is that it should exhibit *keen involvement* in the project and show an obvious *interest* in the outcome (Clemans, 1971). They should establish rapport and give encouragement, thereby projecting positive attitudes and 'pulling along' the respondents. Skilled questionnaire administrators are able to sustain rapport and participant motivation throughout the whole questionnaire completion process.

3.3.5 Communicating the purpose and significance of the survey

Although actions may speak louder than words, this does not mean that words don't matter. An important element in 'selling' the survey to the participants is *communicating* to them the purpose of the survey and conveying to them the potential significance of the results. People tend not to mind answering questions if they see the point. We should also be aware of the fact that, as Gillham (2000) warns us, in our information-conscious age there is a general suspicion that much more data are stored about us than what we know of, and that even 'anonymous' information can be identified. Therefore, unless researchers explain why the information is being collected and how it will be used, some people may be reluctant to complete the questionnaire or to provide true answers even if nothing sensitive is being targeted.

Indeed...

"If respondents are clear about what you are trying to find out and why, they are much more likely to respond appropriately and helpfully, or, indeed, at all. There is a curious convention that if you tell respondents what you are trying to find out, this will 'bias' them. It might simply make them more helpful. If you are mysterious about the purpose of the questionnaire they may be disinclined to answer or misunderstand the purpose, and so bias their answers in that way."

(Gillham, 2000, p. 38)

Just like the cover letter in a postal survey, the introductory speech of the questionnaire administrator needs to be carefully designed. It should briefly cover the following points:

- Introduction.
- The sponsoring organization.
- Purpose of the survey and its potential usefulness.
- Why the particular participants have been selected.
- Assurance of confidentiality.

- The usual duration of completing the questionnaire.
- Any questions?
- Thank you!

A word of caution: The manner in which the questionnaire is presented can have a considerable impact on the participants' performance. By means of illustration, Clemans (1971) reports on a study in which the same test was introduced to three different groups first as an 'intelligence test,' then as an 'achievement test,' and finally as a 'routine test.' Because of the different connotations and inherent motivating characteristics of these three conditions, there was a significant difference between the test results, with the 'intelligence test' group doing best, followed by the 'achievement test group' and finally by the 'routine test' group.

3.3.6 Emphasizing confidentiality

Questionnaires administered in educational settings often contain sensitive items such as the evaluation of the language course (cf. also Sections 2.1.3 and 2.6.3). Students cannot be expected to provide honest information and possibly make critical statements about such issues unless we manage to convince them about the confidentiality of the investigation. Simply saying that the data will be treated confidentially, or making the questionnaires anonymous, may not be a sufficient guarantee for some respondents. In a study that involved the appraisal of a range of situation-specific factors and motives (Clément et al., 1994), we made a big 'fuss' about handing out envelopes to the participants and asking them to put the completed forms in these and then seal them. The administrator, who was external to the school, then stamped every single envelope in front of the students with a university stamp before collecting them. This insured confidentiality.

3.3.7 Questionnaire instructions

It is a general experience in educational psychology that people do not tend to read written directions, and this also applies to the printed instructions of the questionnaire. Therefore, it is advisable for the administrator to read the initial instructions out loud while the respondents read the text silently.

3.3.8 The style and layout of the questionnaire

As argued earlier, respondents are normally willing to spend time and effort on a questionnaire if they believe that they are contributing to a serious investigation. One factor that plays an important role in convincing them about this is the professional quality of the questionnaire. The tone and content of the printed instructions, the layout and typesetting of the items, and small details such as thanking the participants for their cooperation, can all contribute to the formation of a general good impression about the survey, which in turn affects the quality of the responses.

Well said...

"In designing questionnaires it is not merely important for us also to look at things from the respondents' point of view; we must make them *feel* that we are doing so."

(Oppenheim, 1992, p. 122)

Thus, when designing the questionnaire we should not only strive for a psychometrically reliable and valid instrument but also for an *intrinsically involving* one. As Oppenheim (1992) emphasizes, besides eliciting answers, each question also has a covert function to motivate the respondent to continue to cooperate. So, it may be worthwhile sometimes to be a bit more long-winded and instead of giving short prompts such as 'age of starting L2 studies' we could state each question in full, including the word 'please.' Of course, as with so many things in questionnaire construction, a delicate balance needs to be struck here between style and length considerations.

In Section 2.1.2, I argued that attractive layout is an important tool in making the questionnaire engaging. A variety of question styles can make the answering process less monotonous, and an interesting (but not confusing!) variety of graphic features (fonts, spacing) can create a fresh atmosphere. It was mentioned in an earlier section, for example, that a successful strategy someone used was to print documents on thick, beige paper in order for recipients to take them more seriously (Newell, 1993).

3.3.9 Promising feedback on the results

Christopher Ryan (personal communication) has always maintained that survey researchers can do great damage if they pursue what he called a 'slash and burn' strategy. By this he meant that surveyors typically exploit their participants without offering anything in return – as soon as the data have been gathered, they disappear. On the other hand, if someone puts reasonable effort into answering the questions, this involvement will create a natural curiosity about the project and its outcome. It is therefore not only a nice gesture but it also prepares the grounds for future surveys if we offer to send respondents some sort of a feedback on the results (e.g., an article or a copy of the research report). Not everybody will need this, though; in order to avoid any unnecessary waste of paper, we can include a box for people to check if they would like to receive further information. The natural place for this box is somewhere at the end of the questionnaire (cf. Section 2.2.4) but mentioning it at the beginning can serve as an incentive.

Absolutely!

"Remember, if you make a promise to send them something, you really must remember to do it."

(Brown, 2001, p. 87)

3.4 QUESTIONNAIRE ADMINISTRATION, CONFIDENTIALITY, AND OTHER ETHICAL ISSUES

To conclude this chapter on questionnaire administration and data collection, we need to consider aspects which, although unrelated to the psychometric qualities of the measuring instruments, concern the respondents as human beings. The hard fact is that survey research is inherently intrusive and the data we obtain can be abused. Therefore, investigators wishing to adopt this methodology need to be aware of and observe certain basic research ethical principles.

3.4.1 Basic ethical principles of data collection

Drawing on Oppenheim's (1992) and Sudman and Bradburn's (1983) discussion of ethical issues in survey research, the following five principles can be compiled:

Principle 1: No harm should come to the respondents as a result of their participation in the research. This is the primary ethical principle governing data collection and it overrides all other considerations.

Principle 2: The respondent's right to privacy should always be respected, and no undue pressure should be brought to bear. That is, respondents are perfectly within their rights to refuse to answer questions without offering any explanation, and they have the right to decide to whom and under what conditions the information can be made available. No information can be published about identifiable persons or organizations without their permission.

Principle 3: Respondents should be provided with sufficient initial information about the survey to be able to give their informed consent concerning participation and the use of data. The key issue here is what we consider 'sufficient'; I believe that providing true information about the extent to which answers will be held confidential as well as how and for what purpose the data will be used is a minimal requirement. In some contexts the respondents' consent must be confirmed with their signature; however, we should also note that a request for a consent in too formalized a manner can raise undue suspicions that something is not quite right about the survey, and this can reduce the response rate (Sudman & Bradburn, 1983).

Principle 4: In the case of children, permission to conduct the survey should always be sought from some person who has sufficient authority. We will come back to this point in the following section (Section 3.4.2).

Principle 5: It is the researcher's moral and professional (and in some contexts legal) obligation to maintain the level of confidentiality that was promised to the respondents at the onset. We need to make sure that we do not promise a higher degree of confidentiality than what we can achieve.

In many countries, observing these principles is also enforced by legal and institutional requirements. University researchers, for example, may have to submit an application to an Institutional Review Board and their research protocol must be approved of prior to embarking on data collection. In the U.S. these regulations also apply to graduate (MA or PhD) research, and only in exceptional circumstances will Graduate Schools accept a thesis or dissertation without some sort of 'human subjects' approval.

3.4.2 Obtaining parental consent for children

The need for parental consent for including children in a survey is a gray area in many countries. It is my view that unless there exist legal requirements stating otherwise, it may not always be necessary to ask for parental consent when surveying school children. In the case of 'neutral' questionnaires that do not contain any personally sensitive information, permission to conduct the survey can be granted by the children's teachers. Teachers are usually aware of the significance of legal matters and therefore if they have any doubts about who should authorize the project, they will seek advice.

In case parental permission for the research is needed, a common procedure is to send an information leaflet along with a consent form to the children's parents to be signed. In order to avoid cases when the parent has nothing against the survey but simply forgets to return the consent form, a better way to go about this (provided, of course, there are no contradicting legal requirements) is to merely advise the parents about the proposed research and the fact that their child has been chosen (among others) to take part in it, and that parental permission will be assumed *unless the parents object* before the proposed starting date (Oppenheim, 1992).

3.4.3 Strategies for getting around anonymity

We saw in Section 2.1.3 that – from the researcher's point of view – respondent anonymity is often undesirable in survey research because without proper identification we cannot match survey data with other sources of information obtained about the same participants (e.g., course marks or other questionnaires). The other side of the coin, however, is that with certain sensitive questions anonymity may be desirable from the respondents' point of view because they may feel safer this way to provide less self-protective and presumably more accurate answers. Is there a way to 'have the cake and eat it'? That is, can we devise administration procedures that provide the assurance of anonymity and yet produce identifiable data? In the following I will describe two attempts to achieve this objective; one used is my own past research, the other reported in the literature.

Identification through the seating plan

There may be situations when even though you do not promise ano-nymity, you do not want to include the rather salient and potentially loaded task of the respondents identifying themselves by name in the questionnaire. In certain group administration contexts this can be avoided by putting a precoded identification number on each ques-tionnaire and then recording the respondents' exact seating plan during the questionnaire administration (with the help of the students' class teacher, for example). If we hand out the precoded question-naires in a specific order, we will be able to match the code numbers with the respondents' names through the seating plan. In my experi-ence no one has ever complained about, or even raised the issue of, the identification numbers on the questionnaires, and I make it abso-lutely certain that the names remain confidential.

A self-generated identification coding procedure

The identification procedure just described does not ensure anonymity but only saves the salient act of students' writing their name on the questionnaire. A more complex method of ensuring identifiable ano-nymity has been piloted by Kearney et al. (1984) with some success. This method involves students' generating for themselves a unique personal code number and including this on every document they complete – hence the possibility for data linkability. Of course, no one except them would know the identity behind the identification code – hence the assurance of anonymity.

Asking students to make up a code name for themselves has been tried in the past more than once, but the problem with this method is that in longitudinal studies some respondents will almost inevitably have difficulty remembering their ID codes over long intervals. The novel element in Kearney et al.'s (1984) technique is that respondents do not create an imaginary ID code or password but rather generate a code by providing specific code elements that are well known to them but not to the researchers, such as their own or their parents' initials or birth dates, or specific digits of their street addresses or telephone numbers. So, a template for the students' personal identification number would specify each digit separately. This is obviously not an unbreakable code because someone who knows the students well can have access to enough code elements to identify the students, but the procedure works well under many research conditions. There is also the danger of someone not knowing the required information, or some key events in one's life changing (e.g., moving to a new house or when a new brother/sister is born) – and indeed, Kearney et al. report only a 78.1% successful linkage rate for an interval of one year – but the method appears to be reliable for a cross-sectional study that does not involve a long interval between the various data collection procedures.

4

Processing Questionnaire Data

Having designed a questionnaire and administered it to an appropriate sample is half the battle. Now comes the final phase of our research, the processing of the data. The starting point of this phase is the very salient presence of stacks of completed questionnaires taking up what little empty space there is in our office. Accordingly, our initial priority is to get rid of these stacks and transform the information that is hidden in these piles of questionnaires into a more useful form that we can easily store, access, sort, and analyze (Brown, 2001).

Indeed...

"Many books seem to deal with programming for particular statistical analyses, but few detail the painful experience of going from a stack of disorganized hard copy to on-line data that are trustworthy."

(Davidson, 1996, p. ix)

Questionnaire data is most usable if it is stored in a computer file. This is a prerequisite to any professional analysis of the data but even if you are engaged in a small-scale investigation that is not intended to result in a research publication you can save a lot of time if you enter the data into a spreadsheet, for example. Modern computer programs tend to be so user-friendly that one can often learn to use them with less effort than what would be required, for example, to calculate the mean (i.e., the average) scores of the questionnaire responses manually, using a pocket calculator.

This chapter will describe the consecutive steps in processing questionnaire data. We will start with methods of scoring and coding the responses and then entering the data into a computer file. Following this, I will discuss the analysis of closed and open-ended items separately. The chapter will be concluded by summarizing the main types of computer software we can utilize for our research, the most important aspects of reporting questionnaire data, and finally the various ways we can complement our survey data with information obtained from other sources. It may be worth reiterating at this point that this chapter will not elaborate on statistical and qualitative techniques of data analysis. There are excellent books available that survey these procedures (see the *'Further reading'* box at the beginning of Chapter 1).

4.1 CODING QUESTIONNAIRE DATA

Most data analysis software handles data in a numerical rather than in an alphabetic form, and even with programs that allow the storage of information recorded as letters, the procedures that are available for handling such data are limited compared to the vast arsenal of statistical techniques to be used with numerical responses. Therefore, the first step of data processing usually involves converting the respondents' answers to numbers by means of *coding procedures*. As we will see, these procedures are more straightforward with closed-ended questions; processing open-ended questionnaire items requires some sort of *content analysis*.

4.1.1 First things first: Identification code and 'Research Logbook'

Before we get down to actual coding, there are two things to be done. One is compulsory, the other highly recommended.

- The compulsory task is to give each questionnaire a unique *identification code*. In practice this may involve taking each questionnaire one by one and numbering them sequentially by writing a code number in one of the top corners of the front page. Questionnaires coming from the same group (e.g., same school or class) should be kept together and marked with a special code: for example, the first one or two digits of the questionnaire code can refer to the school, the next one to the particular class within the school, and the final numbers identify the individual learners.

- The second task is one that is normally not mentioned in research methodology books. However, years of research experience have convinced me that it is essential to start a formal *'Research Logbook'* at this point. Data analysis will require you to make decisions on an ongoing basis and unless these are properly documented you are likely to soon forget or mix up some of these. As with any real logbook, all the entries should be properly dated and the consecutive pages of the logbook should be numbered and kept together in a folder. Such a logbook will not only help to sort out any emerging confusion but will also contain invaluable recorded information that is readily usable during the writing-up stage (cf. Section 4.6).

4.1.2 The coding frame and the codebook

Having marked each questionnaire with an identification number, we are ready to embark on the *coding* of the items. Except for extensive texts obtained by open-ended questions (which require special content analysis – cf. Section 4.4), the coding process for each item involves converting the answer into a *numerical score*. Because numbers are meaningless themselves and are also easy to mix up, a major element of the coding phase is to compile (a) a *coding frame* that specifies the meaning of the scores for each item and (b) a *codebook* that contains an organized summary of all the coding frames.

The coding frame

The *coding frame* is a classification scheme that offers a numerical score for every possible answer to an item (see Sample 4.2 on page 100). The minimum number of categories is two, as with yes/no questions or gender data: 'Yes' and 'male' are usually coded '1,' whereas 'No' and 'female' are coded '2.' For some open-ended questions (e.g., *What foreign languages have you learned in the past?*) the coding frame can have many more categories – in fact, as many as the number of different answers in all the questionnaires. With such items the coding frame is continuously extended, with every new language mentioned by the respondents being assigned a new number.

The coding frame of every item will need to have a special category for cases when *no answer* has been given (e.g., because someone overlooked the item or intentionally avoided it) – such missing data are often coded '9' or '99' (rather than '0,' which can be confused with several other meanings).

With closed-ended items the coding frame is usually very straightforward: each pre-determined response option is assigned a number (e.g., 'strongly disagree' = 1, 'disagree' = 2, 'neutral' = 3, 'agree' = 4, 'strongly agree' = 5). The coding of open-ended items, however, often goes beyond mechanical conversion and requires a certain amount of subjective interpretation and summary on the part of the coder. Here the task is to condense the detailed information contained in the responses into a limited number of categories; thus, the assigned codes can be seen as shorthand symbols standing for the longer replies (Jolliffe, 1986). Ongoing decisions will need to be made about whether to label two similar but not completely identical responses as the same or whether to mark the difference somehow. For example, if the question concerns preferences for Sunday afternoon leisure activities, it is up to the coder to decide whether 'walking the dog' and 'going for a walk' should be marked the same or not.

Finally, depending on the actual method used to enter the questionnaire data into a computer file, the coding frame may also contain, for each item, a specification of where the information will reside within a computer record (Wilson & McClean, 1994) – this point will be discussed in Section 4.2.

Sample 4.1. Sample coding frames

Have you ever lived in a Spanish-speaking country for more than three months?

Yes = 1; No = 2; missing data = 9

Location: Column 11

* * *

How long have you been learning English?

All answers rounded up to years; minimum value = 01; missing data = 99

Location: Columns 12-13

The codebook

Once the coding of the questionnaire items has been completed and a computer data file has been created (cf. Section 4.2), the questionnaires are usually put into storage and not looked at again (except for special occasions when something needs to be double-checked). Given the general shortage of storage facilities, it is inevitable that sooner or later the questionnaire piles find their way into the trashcan, which will leave the computer file as the only record of the survey data. In order to make these records meaningful for people who have not been involved in creating it, it is worth compiling a *codebook*. This is intended to provide a comprehensive and comprehensible description of the dataset that is accessible to anyone who would like to use it. It usually contains:

- The *name* of each variable that has been entered in the dataset (e.g., 'GENDER,' 'LANGUAGES SPOKEN').

- A brief *description* of the variable and/or the citation of the actual item as it occurred in the questionnaire.

- The *location* of each variable in the computer record (e.g., specified in columns or sequence numbers).

- The *coding frame* for each variable, including the range of valid codes (i.e. minimum and maximum values) and the code used for missing data.

- A note of any *special instructions* or *actions* taken in the course of coding/keying the data (Wilson & McClean, 1994).

The codebook is in many ways related to the *Research Logbook* (cf. Section 4.1.1) and could be, in fact, incorporated into it.

4.2 ENTERING THE DATA INTO A COMPUTER FILE

With the coding frames and the codebook ready, we need to get down to the rather tedious and time-consuming process of keying in the data. All of us involved in survey research have spent countless number of hours in front of a computer screen typing seemingly endless rows of figures. However boring and mechanical this job may be, it is essential that we maintain concentration because every mistyped number will be a contamination of the dataset. In agreement with Brown (2001), I have found that one way of making the task more interesting and more accurate is to work with a partner, taking turns at dictating and typing.

Fred Davidson's plea for backing up data

"Law 1: Back it up.

Law 2: Do it now.

   – Anonymous

I have noticed that nobody seems to learn to back up data until he or she has a serious disaster with data that are personally quite important. Please prove me wrong and abide by these two laws as early in your data career as possible."

(Davidson, 1996, p. 15)

The traditional (and still frequently used) method of entering data into a computer file involves creating a rectangular *text file* (e.g., a word-processing file saved in a "text only with line breaks" file format) in which each horizontal line contains the data from a particular questionnaire and each vertical column (or set of columns) represents a particular variable. For example, Line 1 contains the data from Questionnaire 1, and Columns 1-3 in each line contain a three-digit identification number for the respondent. The final text file would look something like this (note that missing values have been left blank):

```
214 673342 31 5452731 261615 262512 13 423
215 565554 54 545 521 261616 262526 143333
216 542221 21 5661312 251617 152526 134 33
217 474232 43 6352621 472617 261516 133424
218 6 3453 44 5371631 361615 261724 134354
```

This data file is to be accompanied by a special command file which specifies for the computer the content of each column (i.e., which figure represents the score for which variable). During the past decade technology has come a long way and there are now several more user-friendly ways of keying in data; interestingly, some of these still follow the rectangular (rows/columns) format:

- There are various computer spreadsheet programs (such as Excel or Lotus 1-2-3) which allow for setting up rows and columns in an electronic form. These programs can execute certain statistical procedures, and the data entered through them can usually be read, or converted for use, by other, more sophisticated statistical packages.

- 'SPSS,' which is one of the most frequently used statistical packages in the social sciences, has its own Data Editor screen, which provides a convenient, spreadsheet-like method for creating and editing data files.

- One of the main functions of specially designed software for survey research (such as SphinxSurvey; cf. Sections 2.8 and 4.5) is to facilitate data entry. These packages also allow respondents to key in their answers directly, following an on-line version of the questionnaire (which means that no hard copy of the questionnaire record is created).

- Some specialist programs even allow structuring the computer screen to look like the original questionnaire. This can make the link between the hard copy and the electronic file more straightforward, which helps to reduce any typing errors.

4.3 PROCESSING CLOSED QUESTIONS

Closed-ended questions are the most common types of questionnaire items. The complete processing sequence of such questions involves a number of consecutive steps, starting with the initial data check and cleaning, and concluded by the statistical analyses of the data.

4.3.1 Data cleaning

The initial data file will always contain mistakes. Some of these are the result of human error occurring during the data entry phase (e.g., typing the wrong number) and some are mistakes made by the respondent when filling in the questionnaire. *Data cleaning* involves correcting as many of these errors and inaccuracies as possible before the actual analyses are undertaken. The main checks and techniques are as follows:

- *Correcting impossible data.* Most items have a specific range, determined by the given response options or by the inherent logic of the item. A quick frequency listing of all the items can expose out-of-range values; for example, with a six-point Likert-scale a value of 7 is obviously incorrect, and if someone's age is entered as 110, we can also suspect human inaccuracy. Once such impossible values have been detected, we need to check the hard copy of the particular questionnaires, and then enter the correct values.

- *Correcting incorrectly entered values that conform to the permissible range.* It is easy to detect and correct a value of 7 with a six-point Likert-scale. But what about a typing error in the same scale when '5' has been recorded instead of '4'? The only way of detecting such a mistake is by means of a very laborious procedure, whereby the entire data bank is reentered in a second data file and then the two data files (which ought to be identical) are computer-checked for correspondence with each other.

- *Correcting contradicting data.* Some questionnaires have 'routed' items, which means that some questions are to be answered only if the respondent gave a particular answer to a previous question. For example, if a language learner gives a negative answer to the question *"Have you ever stayed in the L2 environment for an extended period?"* and then answers '6 months' to the subsequent *If so, for how long?"* question, something is obviously wrong. Depending on the type of questions asked, several other logical checks are also conceivable. In any case, when such inconsistencies are found, a closer inspection of the questionnaire can usually help us to remedy these, but sometimes the only way of getting rid of the contamination is to eliminate both parts of the contradicting or illogical combination.

- *Examining implausible data.* The data check may highlight values that are inconsistent with the rest of the dataset, for example, because they are way out of the usual range. If such 'suspicious' values are not merely the result of a typing error, they are referred to as '*outliers.*' They can indicate an out-of-the-ordinary but true response but they can also be caused by respondent carelessness or intentional silliness (which does happen with some participants). If a close analysis of the response patterns in the particular questionnaire points to one of the latter two options, we should consider eradicating the spurious information so that it does not bias the results. If we cannot make an unambiguous decision, we may conduct the main analysis twice, with and without the outlier, and see if the outcome will provide a clue about how to handle the outlier.

4.3.2 Data manipulation

Data manipulation involves making changes in the dataset prior to the analyses in order to make it more appropriate for certain statistical procedures; it does *not* involve biasing the results one way or another.

Handling missing data

One issue that should definitely be resolved before the analyses is deciding what to do with missing values. They are a nuisance in many ways. First, it is not always clear whether the lack of any useful response is meaningful or not. For example, if Rupert is asked about what foreign languages he speaks and he leaves the question unanswered, would this mean that (a) Rupert only speaks his mother tongue, or (b) he has skipped the question by mistake, or (c) he has intentionally refused to answer?

Second, for the purpose of certain statistical procedures a single missing value can invalidate an otherwise complete questionnaire. For example, in multivariate statistics when many variables are examined at the same time, some programs (e.g., AMOS, a well-known program used for structural equation modeling) can set it as a basic require-ment to have valid values for *every* variable for a person, or the person will be automatically excluded from the analyses. Given that, regrettably, it is quite common to have a few missing values in every questionnaire, we can end up losing as much as half of our sample this way, which is clearly undesirable. In such cases the program might offer some ways of imputing the missing data that are unlikely to change the results, for example by including item means or maxi-mum likelihood estimates. Luckily, several statistical procedures allow for a choice between *listwise deletion* and *pairwise deletion*: The former refers to the 'hard' line whereby one missing value deletes a whole case from all the analyses even if some of the available data could be used for certain calculations. The latter refers to the tempo-rary deletion of a case from the analysis only when specific statistics are computed that would involve the particular missing value.

In sum, missing data are always something to bear in mind and it is advisable to go through all our variables prior to the statistical analyses to check whether missing values have been properly re-corded and interpreted. If we have '0' values coded, we would also need to consider whether these should be assigned a missing value status.

Recoding values

It has been recommended earlier (in Section 2.6.2) that in order to avoid a response set where the respondents mark only one side of a rating scale, it is worth including in the questionnaire both positively and negatively worded items; this may also reduce the harmful effects of the acquiescence bias. However, if we have such negatively worded items, we must not forget to reverse the scoring for these before including them in multi-item scales. This may sound like an obvious and trivial recommendation, but unless you make the recoding of such scores a compulsory step before any real analyses, it is all too easy to forget about it.

Standardizing the data

When we use pooled results from various subsamples, one way of controlling for the heterogeneous nature of the subgroups is to use standardized scores. The standardization of raw scores involves the conversion of the distribution within a sample in a way that the mean will be 0 and the standard deviation 1. Thus, standard scores express how much each raw value is different from the subgroup mean, and by equalizing the means, scores obtained from different subsamples (e.g., different classes in the school) are readily comparable. Such a transformation is permissible with correlation-based analyses (e.g., correlation analysis, factor analysis, discriminant analysis and structural equation modeling) because when we compute correlations we can carry out certain mechanical conversions of the raw scores without these affecting the resulting coefficients. For a detailed argument in favor of standardizing heterogeneous questionnaire data, see Gardner (1985, pp. 78-80); he also provides a hypothetical illustration in which a motivation measure shows significant positive correlation with learning achievement in two school classes when computed separately, but the same correlation becomes non-significant when the data are pooled without standardization.

4.3.3 Reducing the number of variables in the questionnaire

Once we have completed data cleaning and data manipulation, we are ready to embark on the examination of the obtained data. The first step in analyzing questionnaire data is always to *reduce to manageable proportions the number of variables* measured by the questionnaire so that the mass of details does not prevent us from seeing the forest through the trees. The rationale for this is that – in accordance with the arguments in Section 2.3.2 – a well-designed questionnaire contains multiple items focused on each content area and therefore the parallel items need to be summed up in *multi-item scales* for the purpose of analysis. However, even if we have not consciously devised multiple items assessing the same target, the chances are that some questions will tap into the same underlying trait and will therefore have to be summed.

The procedure to compute a multi-item scale is simple: all it takes is to calculate the mean of the constituent items. The difficult part is to decide *which* items to merge. Most researchers apply one of two approaches (or a combination of these) to determine which items belong together:

- Based on the theoretical considerations guiding the construction of the questionnaire, we form clusters of items that are hypothesized to hang together and then conduct an internal consistency check (cf. Section 4.3.5) to determine whether our assumptions are born out in practice. As we will see in Section 4.3.5, some modern computer software can even advise us about the desirability of excluding one or more items from the scales.

- One statistical technique, *factor analysis*, is particularly suited to reduce the number of variables to a few values that still contain most of the information found in the original variables (Hatch & Lazaraton, 1991). Although the procedure is rather complex mathematically, it is straightforward conceptually: It explores the interrelationships of the items and tries to find patterns of correspondence – that is, common underlying themes – among them. The outcome is a small set of underlying dimensions, referred to as *factors* or *components*. This 'pattern finding capacity' makes factor analysis very useful in making large data sets more manageable and therefore it is often used in the preparatory phase in data processing.

4.3.4 Main types of questionnaire data

Although questionnaires show a great variety, they elicit only four main types of data: *nominal* (categorical), *ordinal, interval*, and *textual*. As will be discussed in Section 4.4, the last type – open-ended and sometimes extensive verbal response – is usually converted to quantifiable categories, that is, to one of the first three data types. The main difference between the three types of quantitative data lies in the precision of the measurement:

- *Nominal* or *categorical data* come from scales that have no numerical value, such as gender or race. Here the assigned values are completely arbitrary; for example, for the gender variable male is usually coded '1' and female '2,' which does not indicate any difference in size or salience.

- *Ordinal data* are similar to nominal data except that greater numbers refer to the order of the values on a continuum. In other words, ordinal data involves ranked numbers. For example, a multiple-choice item with options such as 'once a day,' 'once a week,' 'once a month,' 'once a year,' and 'never' will produce ordinal data because the answers can be placed on a 'frequency' continuum.

- *Interval data* can be seen as ordinal data in which the various values are at an equal distance – or intervals – from each other on a continuum. That is, equal numerical differences in the coding imply equal differences in the degree/salience/size of the variable being measured. An example of such data would be L2 proficiency test scores.

The separation of these three types of measure becomes important when we select the statistical techniques to be used with our data. Certain types of data can be analyzed only by means of certain types of techniques: The big dividing line is between *parametric procedures*, which require interval data, and *non-parametric procedures* which can be applied to ordinal and even nominal data. Statistical computer packages contain a variety of procedures belonging to both types.

4.3.5 Examining the reliability and validity of the data

Reliability and *validity* are two key concepts in measurement theory, referring to the psychometric properties of the measurement techniques and the data obtained by them.

- The *reliability* of a psychometric instrument refers to the extent to which scores on the instrument are free from errors of measurement. For example, bathroom scales are not reliable if they show different figures depending on how steamy the air in the bathroom is, and neither are proficiency test raters if their evaluation varies according to how tired they are.

- *Validity* is the extent to which a psychometric instrument measures what it has been designed to measure. For example, if a test that is claimed to assess overall language proficiency measures only grammatical knowledge, the test is not valid in terms of evaluating communicative competence, although it may be perfectly valid with regard to the appraisal of grammar (in which case it should be called a grammar test).

Because of the salience of these terms in educational and psychological measurement, tens of thousands of pages have been written about them and every research manual will provide a detailed discussion about how to compute reliability/validity indices.

Questionnaires are measurement instruments and, accordingly, they too must possess adequate reliability and validity. Standardized questionnaires need to undergo rigorous validation procedures and the manuals usually present a variety of reliability and validity coefficients. For made-to-measure research instruments that we develop for our specific purpose, however, it is not always feasible to provide indices of every aspect of validity and reliability. Yet, even in cases where there are no resources and opportunities for elaborate validation exercises, we should strive for a questionnaire that has appropriate and well-documented reliability in at least one aspect: *internal consistency*. This attribute refers to the homogeneity of the items making up the various multi-item scales within the questionnaire. If your instrument has it, you can feel fairly safe.

Internal consistency reliability

In order to meet internal consistency reliability requirements, a questionnaire must satisfy two conditions:

- Instead of single items, *multi-item scales* (cf. Section 2.3.2) are to be used wherever it is possible.

- Multi-item scales are only effective if the items work together in a homogeneous manner, that is, if they measure the same target area. In psychometric terms this means that each item on a scale should correlate with the other items and with the total scale score, which has been referred to as Likert's criterion of 'Internal Consistency' (Anderson, 1985).

Internal consistency is generally seen as the psychometric prerequuisite for any scientific survey measurement. It does not guarantee the validity of a scale – as in extreme cases we can imagine a scale where all the items consistently measure something different from the scale's intended purpose – but the intuitive contention is that if several items *seem* to measure a construct and they can be proven to measure the *same thing*, then this 'same thing' *must be* the targeted construct.

Nunnally (1978) points out that the term 'internal consistency' is partly a misnomer, because the reliability coefficient is based not only on the average correlation among the items (i.e., internal consistency proper) but also on the number of items making up the scale. That is, it is much easier to achieve appropriate internal consistency reliability with 20 items than with 3. This, of course, makes good sense: with few items the wording of the individual items can make much more of a difference than with 20, and therefore short scales need to display more evidence of homogeneity than long ones to be seen as trustworthy. Although internal consistency admittedly covers only one aspect of overall reliability, Nunnally concludes that reliability estimated from internal consistency is usually surprisingly close to the reliability estimated from other sources, for example from correlations between alternative questionnaire forms.

Measuring and ensuring internal consistency reliability

Internal consistency reliability is measured by the *Cronbach Alpha coefficient* (named after its introducer, L. J. Cronbach). This is a figure ranging between zero and +1, and if it proves to be very low, either the particular scale is too short or the items have very little in common. Internal consistency estimates for well-developed attitude scales containing as few as 10 items ought to approach 0.80. Because of the complexity of the second language acquisition process, L2 researchers typically want to measure many different areas in one questionnaire, and therefore cannot use very long scales (or the completion of the questionnaire would take several hours). This means that somewhat lower Cronbach Alpha coefficients are to be expected, but even with short scales of 3-4 items we should aim at reliability coefficients in excess of 0.70; if the Cronbach Alpha of a scale does not reach 0.60, this should sound warning bells.

How do we obtain Cronbach Alpha coefficients? Modern statistical computer programs make it relatively easy to conduct item analysis. The 'Reliability' procedure of SPSS, for example, not only provides the Cronbach Alpha for any given scale but also computes what the alpha coefficient would be if a particular item were deleted from the scale. By looking at the list of these 'would-be' alphas for each item, we can immediately see which item reduces the internal consistency of the scale and should therefore be considered for omission. Sample 4.2 presents the results of the analysis of a 7-item scale focusing on *group cohesiveness*. The Cronbach Alpha coefficient of the total scale is 0.77, which is rather good. However, if we look at the alpha statistics if each item were to be deleted, we can see that deleting Item 1 would add to the internal consistency of the scale, whereas deleting any of the other items would reduce the reliability.

An alternative method for making scales homogeneous is using factor analysis to help to eliminate items (see, for example, Noels, Pelletier, Clément, & Vallerand, 2000, who followed this procedure). In this case, scale uni-dimensionality is achieved by selecting only those items that have the highest loadings on the factor that they were written to tap. Finally, the simplest and yet effective way of ensuring that the items making up a scale belong together is to compute correlation coefficients for each item with the total scale score and to retain the items with the highest correlations. Sample 4.2 shows very clearly that the item-total correlation for Item 1 is considerably lower than all the other correlations, which confirms the result of the reliability analysis, namely that the internal consistency of this scale would improve if this item was deleted.

Sample 4.2. Reliability analysis for "Group Cohesiveness"

ITEM-TOTAL STATISTICS (based on real data)

Item	Corrected item-total correlation	Cronbach Alpha if item deleted
1. Sometimes there are tensions among the members of my group and these make learning more difficult.	.23	.80
2. Compared to other groups like mine, I feel that my group is better than most	.50	.75
3. There are some cliques in this group.	.44	.76
4. If I were to participate in another group like this one, I would want it to include people who are very similar to the ones in this group	.63	.72
5. This group is composed of people who fit together.	.66	.72
6. There are some people in this group who do not really like each other.	.47	.75
7. I am dissatisfied with my group.	.58	.73

Cronbach Alpha for the 7 items = .77

4.3.6 Statistical procedures to analyze data

The standard method of analyzing quantitative questionnaire data is by means of submitting them to various statistical procedures. These involve a range of different techniques, from calculating item score means on a pocket calculator to running complex statistical analyses. As mentioned earlier, it is beyond the scope of this book to provide a detailed analysis of the available procedures. Instead, I would like to emphasize one crucial aspect of statistical data analysis that is so often misunderstood or ignored by novice researchers: the distinction between *descriptive statistics* and *inferential statistics*.

Descriptive statistics

Descriptive statistics are used to summarize sets of numerical data in order to conserve time and space. It is obvious that providing the *mean* and the *range* (i.e., minimum and maximum values) of a variable is a more professional way of describing the respondents' answers than listing all the scores that have been obtained. And if we also include the *standard deviation* of the results (which is an index of the average disparity among the scores), we have achieved a well-rounded description of the scores that would satisfy most purposes. Thus, descriptive statistics offer a tidy way of presenting the data we have. The important thing, however, is to note that these statistics do *not* allow drawing any general conclusions that would go beyond the sample. In practice this means that we ought to start every sentence which describes descriptive features by *'In my sample....'* If you want to say something about possible general lessons that may be drawn from your study – which is what we usually do when we write a journal article or give a conference presentation – you need to compute *inferential statistics*.

Inferential statistics

Descriptive statistics are useful, for example, to describe the achievement of a particular class of learners. What happens, however, if we notice that, say, the L2 learning achievement of boys and girls shows a remarkable difference in our sample, with girls outperforming boys (which is often the case)? Can we draw the inference that girls are better language learners? No. Based on descriptive statistics all we can say is that in this class girls did better than boys. In order to venture any generalization concerning the wider population and not just the particular sample, we need to show that the difference between girls and boys is *significant in the statistical sense*. To achieve this, we need to employ *inferential statistical procedures*.

Well said...

"When an individual uses descriptive statistics, he talks about the data he has; but with *inferential statistics*, he talks about data he does not have."

(Popham & Sirotnik, 1973, p. 40)

Statistical significance denotes whether a particular result is powerful enough to indicate a more generalizable phenomenon. If a result is non-significant, this means that we cannot be certain that it did not occur in the particular sample only because of chance (e.g., because of the unique composition of the learners examined). In other words, even if we feel that the particular descriptive data reveal some true and more general tendencies, we cannot exclude the possibility of a mere coincidence. For this reason, statistically non-significant results *must be ignored* in research studies.

One important feature of statistical significance is that it is the function of not only the magnitude of the result but also the *size of the sample* investigated. It is easy to see why this is so: If we assess, say, millions of people, even a relatively weak tendency can be regarded as typical of the whole population, whereas with only a handful of people we cannot be certain about far stronger tendencies. Therefore, computers take the combined effect of magnitude and sample size into account when they calculate the significance of a result. If they mark a particular result as *significant*, we can utter a sigh of relief as this means that the observed phenomenon represents a significant departure from what might be expected by chance alone. That is, it can be assumed to be *real*.

To sum it up, if researchers have some interesting data obtained from, say, a language class and they want to use these data as the basis for making certain more general claims, it is not enough to merely quote descriptive statistics that support their observation. They also have to run inferential statistical tests to check if what they have noticed is powerful enough to qualify as being statistically significant.

4.4 CONTENT ANALYSIS OF OPEN-ENDED QUESTIONS

Although it was argued in Sections 1.3 and 2.5 that wide-open, essay-like questions do not work well in questionnaires and therefore should be avoided, questions that are slightly 'less open' can have some merits and are well worth experimenting with as long as this does not exist at the expense of the closed questions (in terms of response time or willingness). Because open-ended questions do not have precoded response options, their processing is less straightforward than that of closed items.

'*Specific open questions*' (cf. Section 2.5.1) usually ask about factual information that is easy to summarize. With an adequate coding frame (cf. Section 4.1.2), the responses to these items can be coded into distinct categories and then treated as nominal, or possibly ordinal, data (cf. Section 4.3.4).

With *clarification questions, sentence completion tasks*, and *short-answer questions* (cf. Sections 2.5.2 to 2.5.4), the categorization process involves more potentially subjective elements on the part of the coder. In order to avoid the harmful effects of such rater subjectivity, these items are to be processed by means of some systematic 'content analysis,' whereby the pool of diverse responses is reduced to a handful of key issues in a reliable manner. This is usually achieved through a stepwise process that involves two broad phases (for a detailed discussion, see Brown, 2001):

1. Taking each person's response in turn and marking in them any distinct content elements, substantive statements, or key points.

2. Based on the ideas and concepts highlighted in the texts (cf. Phase 1), forming broader categories to describe the content of the response in a way that allows for comparisons with other responses.

The categories obtained in Phase 2 can be numerically coded and then entered into the data file to be treated as quantitative data. Some of the key points highlighted in Phase 1 can also be quoted verbatim for the purpose of illustration and exemplification, or to retain some of the original flavor of the response.

Finally, although often omitted, qualitative data can also be checked for reliability, for example by computing intercoder agreement coefficients that describe to what extent two raters agree on assigning categories to the responses (see Brown, 2001, pp. 231-240).

Well said...

"In practice, even the most simple forms of content analysis involve a good deal of to-ing and fro-ing and there are almost always some loose ends, unclassifiable elements which have to be reported as such."

(Gillham, 2000, p. 65)

4.5 COMPUTER PROGRAMS FOR PROCESSING QUESTIONNAIRE DATA

There are numerous statistical software packages that can be used to process quantitative questionnaire data. Personally, I have always used, and been satisfied with, 'SPSS' (Statistical Package for the Social Sciences), which is one of the market leaders in this category. There are also various computer programs to facilitate the qualitative analysis of transcribed texts (e.g., NUD*IST, NVivo).

From a survey researcher's point of view, programs that can handle quantitative and qualitative questionnaire data in an integrated manner are particularly valuable. As described in Section 2.8, there are over 30 available desktop packages specifically created to combine questionnaire design, data collection, and qualitative/quantitative data analysis (for references, see Section 2.8). Although currently they show considerable variation in terms of the elaborateness of the various processing components, many packages can already perform most of what ordinary users will ever need. Furthermore, developments in this area are so fast that the improved versions available in a few years' time will have ironed out most of the currently existing shortcomings.

In Section 2.8, I introduced one particular program, *SphinxSurvey*, which is an integrated, PC-based Windows package for conducting questionnaire-based surveys (for a review, see Macer, 1999). One reason for selecting this software has been its unique and powerful qualitative data analysis module. All the available survey research programs on the market can perform standard statistical operations (and for advanced statistics, researchers can switch over to a specialized statistical software), but there is far less available in terms of analyzing the open-ended, longer verbal responses. The lexical module of *SphinxSurvey* provides a variety of indices about open responses, ranging from total number of words and the number of unique words, to the most frequently used words and lexical range. The program can reduce the vocabulary of each response by eliminating non-relevant words and terms, leaving a core lexicon that is readily analyzable for content. Other sophisticated functions offer *computer aided content analysis* of each text response by assigning categories to it, which can then be analyzed by means of quantitative methods. Such lexical examinations are still fairly novel in survey research and are definitely worth experimenting with.

4.6 SUMMARIZING AND REPORTING QUESTIONNAIRE DATA

Survey data can be used for a great variety of purposes and each of these might require somewhat different types of summaries and reports of the findings. It is obvious, for instance, that a PhD dissertation will have to meet criteria that are very different from the presentation requirements of a summary of student achievement at a school staff meeting. Rather than attempting to provide templates for all the diverse applications (such templates are readily available in various writers' manuals), in the following I will focus on three general aspects of survey reports:

- *General guidelines* about what to report and how.
- The *technical information* about the survey that needs to be included in a professional report to accompany the actual findings.
- *Presentation methods* that can make the data more reader-friendly and digestible.

4.6.1 General guidelines

There are two problem areas in reporting survey findings that I have often observed both in my own and my graduate students' writing: (a) the question of how much one should be allowed to generalize; and (b) the problem of the detached nature of the largely quantitative summaries from the real-life situations they concern.

How much to generalize

With regard to the issue of generalizing, it is so easy to offer the broad and rather unhelpful guideline: *Do not overgeneralize!* However, research in most cases is all about the need to produce generalizable findings. After all, with the exception of 'action research,' researchers in the L2 field rarely investigate a sample with the sole purpose of wanting to know more only about the particular people under investigation. Instead, what we normally want to do is find out more about the *population* (cf. Section 3.1), that is, about all the similar people in the world. This means that the crucial question to decide is what 'over' means in the term 'overgeneralization.'

It would again be easy to give a less-than-useful, though technically correct, definition of 'overgeneralization,' namely that it occurs when we generalize the findings to a population that our sample is not representative of. This states, in effect, that if we examine, say, primary school pupils, we should not generalize our findings to secondary or university students. There is no question about the validity of this claim, and yet it avoids the crux of the problem, which is that if we were to observe this guideline too closely, few (if any) studies in the educational psychological literature could speak about 'students' in general. It is clear that hardly any investigations are sufficiently large-scale to include representatives of every main age group, ethnicity, school type, and subject matter in a single study (just to list four key factors) – yet the discussions of the findings are rarely restricted to the particular subpopulation in question.

Having said this, I still believe that we should beware of overgeneralizations, but in the absence of hard and fast rules about what constitutes *'over'*-generalization, we need to strive to find a delicate balance between the following two considerations:

- On the one hand, we may wish to be able to say something of a broader relevance (since it may severely reduce our audience if we limit our discussion to very specific subgroups).

- On the other hand, big claims can usually be made only on the basis of big studies.

Having said these, some classic studies in the research literature did confine their focus to extremely limited target issues, and some famous big claims were indeed made based on small studies... So, the only conclusion I can offer is that researchers need to exercise great caution when pitching the level of generalization in their research reports.

Detachment from real life

Researchers often note how ironical it is that months of hard labor can sometimes be summarized in one or two tables. While this may not be a problem in basic research – after all, Einstein's theory of relativity did not exactly take up several volumes either – in more applied studies when we are looking at concrete questions concerning real people, a primarily quantitative summary may lose some of the edge and flavor of the original issue. This is when a few open-ended items in the questionnaire might play a useful role in providing quotations that can help to retain or restore the real perspective. Furthermore, as Moser and Kalton (1971) remind us, to many readers, statistical tables are dull and difficult to comprehend, and a certain amount of verbatim quotation of answers can effectively enliven the report (cf. also Section 4.6.3, which describes a number of reader-friendly presentation techniques).

How true...!

"If the basic research questions are complex (when are they not?) then your data are going to look pretty thin and superficial if all you can report are the results of a questionnaire. In a small-scale study this lack is going to be particularly apparent."

(Gillham, 2000, p. 81)

4.6.2 Technical information to accompany survey results

Novice researchers often make the mistake of concentrating only on the presentation of their actual findings in their survey reports. While this approach may appear logical, it fails to take into account the fact that in order to be able to interpret (and believe) the claims made, readers will have to be convinced that the methodology used to produce the particular findings was appropriate. This does not mean that we can only report results if our study did not have any methodological limitations but only that we must provide a concise and yet detailed summary of the main aspects of the survey, including any known limiting factors. There is no perfect study and it is up to the readers (and the journal editors) to decide on the value of the findings. The following list of the main points to be covered can be used as a checklist:

PARTICIPANTS (i.e., the sample)

➢ *Description of the sample*; the exact details to be supplied depend on the focus of the study but normally include as a minimum the participants':

- total number (possibly accompanied by some justification and the total number of all the eligible people),
- age,
- gender,
- ethnicity,
- any grouping variable (e.g., number of courses or classes they come from),
- level of L2 proficiency,
- L2 learning history,
- L2 teaching institution (if applicable),
- type of tuition received.

➤ Any necessary *additional details* (again, depending on the study), such as:

- general aptitude (or academic ability),
- socioeconomic background,
- participants' occupation or (if the participants are students) areas of specialization,
- L2 class size,
- L2 teaching materials used,
- amount of time spent in an L2 host environment.

➤ The *sampling method* used for the selection of the participants.

➤ If the sample consisted of several groups: *similarities* and *differences* among them.

QUESTIONNAIRE

➤ *Description* of and *rationale* for the main content areas covered.

➤ *Justification* of why some potentially important areas have been left out.

➤ *Factual description* of the instrument (with the actual questionnaire possibly attached in the Appendix), including:

- number of main parts/sections,
- number of items,
- types of items (e.g., response types),
- scoring procedures.

➤ Details about the *piloting* of the instrument.

➤ Any available data concerning the *reliability* and *validity* of the instrument.

➤ Details about how *confidentiality/anonymity* was handled.

QUESTIONNAIRE ADMINISTRATION

➤ *Procedures* used to administer the questionnaire, including:

- any advance information provided,
- characteristics of the questionnaire administrator(s) (including training/briefing, role, experience, education, etc.)
- administration format (e.g., postal; one-to-one on-the-spot; one-to-one take-away; group)
- any special circumstances or events.

➤ *Length of time* that was needed to complete all questionnaires.

➤ *Duration of the complete survey* (if it included several administration dates).

➤ Questionnaire *return rate*.

VARIABLES

➤ *Complete list* of the variables derived from the raw questionnaire data, including details of how they were operationalized.

➤ With *multi-item scales*: the number of constituent items and the Cronbach Alpha internal consistency reliability coefficient for each scale.

LIMITATIONS

➤ Any *circumstances* (foreseen or unforeseen) that may have affected the results in a systematic manner.

➤ Problems related to the *size* and *representativeness* of the sample.

➤ Any potential *biases of the sample* (related to composition, selection procedure, nonparticipation, or drop-out rate, etc.).

➤ *Biases* stemming from missing *data*.

➤ Problems with the *research design*.

Well said...

"Research workers writing for fellow scientists are generally careful to emphasize limitations; indeed they sometimes fall over backwards to argue that what they have been doing is worthless. But particularly when writing for a general audience, the temptation to soft-pedal limitations is strong; the writer feels that the significance of technical shortcomings will not be appreciated, and shortage of space further encourages him to skip them. There is little need to stress how serious such omissions can be."

(Moser & Kalton, 1971, p. 477)

4.6.3 Reader-friendly data presentation methods

Questionnaire studies typically produce a wealth of data, and therefore developing effective and digestible – i.e., reader-friendly – ways of presenting the data is an essential skill for the survey researcher. A rule of thumb is that we should present as much of the information as possible in *figures* and *tables* rather than in the running text. Or, to go one step further: whatever can be presented in tables and figures, should be.

Figures

Figures are methods to visualize various characteristics of the data. I have used two types of figures in the past, *charts/diagrams* and *schematic representations*.

Charts/diagrams offer a useful way of describing the size/strength of variables in relation to each other. *Bar charts* and *line charts* use a vertical Y-axis and a horizontal X-axis to present data (see Figures 1 and 2). The vertical axis usually represents the unit of measurement (or dependent variable) and the horizontal axis the independent variable(s). These charts are very flexible in terms of the type of data they can display, and they can effectively demonstrate comparisons or changes over time in a way that is easy to interpret (Fink, 1995).

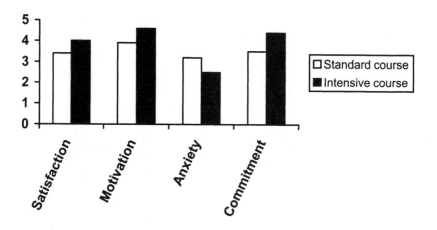

Figure 1. Sample bar chart

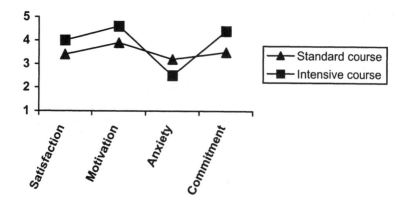

Figure 2. Sample line chart

Pie charts are used to describe proportions and percentages. The first pie chart in Figure 3 can display, for example, the proportion of focusing on three L2 skills in a language course. If we want to highlight changes, we can use two pies. Thus, the second pie below can be seen, for example, to represent the revised curriculum after some significant educational reform. By changing the overall size of the second pie we can also indicate growth or shrinkage (Fink, 1995) – the pie charts in Figure 3 may suggest a decrease in the total amount of tuition after the reform.

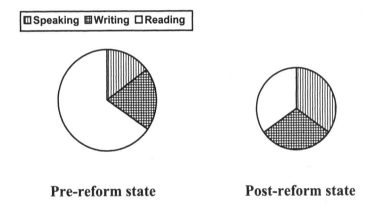

Pre-reform state　　　　　**Post-reform state**

Figure 3. Sample pie charts

Schematic representations offer a useful way to describe complex relationships between multiple variables, and typically utilize various boxes and arrows (see Figure 4). They can be used, for example, to describe the blueprint of mental processes or the componential structure of multi-level constructs.

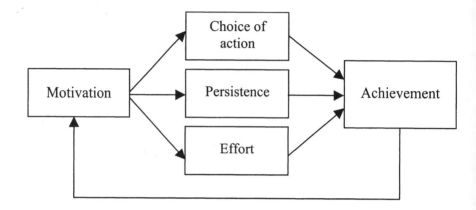

Figure 4. Sample schematic representation

Tables

Tables are used to summarize data about the respondents and their responses, and to present results of statistical analyses (see Sample 4.2 on page 113, and Sample Table 1 on page 129). They are typically made up of rows and columns of numbers, each marked with headings and subheadings. They can provide a more accurate and richer description than figures but they are less digestible because they lack the advantage of a visual impact. Tables are, therefore, more appropriate for articles in academic journals than for lectures to a non-specialist audience.

4.7 COMPLEMENTING QUESTIONNAIRE DATA WITH OTHER INFORMATION

Having discussed how to construct and administer questionnaires, and then how to analyze and report the responses we have obtained, the final section of this book addresses ways of proceeding toward a

Sample Table 1. Descriptive statistics of the content of this book

	Frequency		
	Pages	**Boxes**	**Words**
Introduction	2	1	620
Chapter 1	13	4	3,455
Chapter 2	54	22	14,495
Chapter 3	26	6	7,293
Chapter 4	36	8	9,389
Conclusion	5	0	995

fuller understanding of the content area targeted by our survey. As discussed in Chapter 1, although questionnaires offer a versatile and highly effective means of data collection, the kinds of insight they can generate are limited by several factors, most notably by the restricted time and effort respondents are usually willing to invest in completing the instrument. In a more general sense, questionnaires are also limited by the shortcomings of quantitative research as a methodological approach, in that they offer little scope for explorative, in-depth analyses of complex relationships or for doing justice to the subjective variety of an individual life.

The good news about questionnaires, however, is that their flexible nature makes them ideal to be used in complex research paradigms in concert with other data collection methods. Brown (2001), for example, argues that questionnaire data and interview data can be seen as inherently complementary:

> ... in the sense that interviews are more suitable for exploring what the questions are and questionnaires are more suitable for answering those questions. Sometimes, you may want to use the

strengths of both types of instruments in a single survey project. (pp. 78-79)

Such an approach can be labeled as a *"two-phase design,"* made up of separate qualitative and quantitative phases (Creswell, 1994): it allows the main theses of a qualitative project to be tested in a survey study in order to determine the distribution and frequency of the phenomena that have been uncovered.

In a similar vein, Gillham (2000) urges survey researchers to conduct semi-structured interviews to accompany questionnaire results in order to gain a better understanding of what the numerical responses actually mean. Interview data can both illustrate and illuminate questionnaire results and can "bring your research study to life" (p. 82). Indeed, questionnaires lend themselves to follow-up *retrospective research* (for recent discussions of 'stimulated recall' techniques, see Gass & Mackey, 2000; Kasper, 1998; Kormos, 1998) in which participants are asked to go through their own responses with an interviewer and provide retrospective comments on the reason for their particular answer in each item. Thus, in this design the participant's own item responses serve as prompts for further open-ended reflection and, at the same time, the coverage of all the items ensures systematicity and comprehensiveness.

Reversing the process, questionnaires can also be used in the preparatory phase of a qualitative interview study in sampling the interviewees systematically. One general concern about interview studies is the somewhat *ad hoc* nature of participant selection; however, this concern could be eliminated by applying another type of *two-phase design* in which the first phase involves the administration of a short questionnaire to a substantial sample, and on the basis of the responses the researcher identifies certain individuals who represent either typical or extreme cases from certain key aspects of the study. These people will then be invited to participate in the second, qualitative interview phase.

Finally, we should also note that although in this section I have only described the application of questionnaires in qualitative-quantitative 'mixed methodology' designs (because I believe that this combination has great potential for future research as it can bring out the best of both approaches while neutralizing the shortcomings and biases inherent in each paradigm), survey questionnaires can be integrated into several other research methods, for example to collect background information about the participants in an experimental study or to complement classroom observation data. In fact, the recent advocacy of the integrated use of multiple data collection methods, in line with the general concept of 'triangulation,' has created a fertile ground for the increased use of professionally designed questionnaires as psychometrically sound measuring instruments.

Conclusion and Checklist

The previous four chapters have provided a summary of question-naire theory. Hopefully, they have also made a strong case for basing questionnaire design and processing on scientific principles rather than merely on the researcher's common sense. As emphasized in the Introduction, this book has been intended to serve practical purposes and therefore in this concluding section I will draw up a checklist of what I consider the most important points and recommendations for every phase of the questionnaire survey. Good luck with your future questionnaires!

CONSTRUCTING THE QUESTIONNAIRE

1. Only in exceptional cases should a questionnaire be more than 4 pages long and take more than 30 minutes to complete; if access to the participants is restricted to a certain amount of time, set the maximum length of the questionnaire with the slowest readers in mind so that everybody can finish within the given period.

2. When deciding on the questionnaire content, start by generating a theoretically driven list of the main areas to be covered.

3. Avoid the use of single-item variables; instead, include minimum 3-4 items addressing every content area.

4. Avoid truly open-ended questions that require lengthy answers.

5. Keep the number of items that are seeking confidential information to the minimum.

6. Be careful about how you formulate sensitive items (for specific guidelines, see Section 2.6.3).

7. Try and make the starter questions particularly involving.

8. Make sure that the questionnaire has a clear, logical, and well-marked structure.

9. Personal/factual questions about the respondent should go to the end.

10. Open-ended questions are the least intrusive if they are toward the end.

11. When writing items, observe the following:

    - The best items are often the ones that sound as if they had been said by someone.

    - Short items written in simple and natural language are good items.

    - Avoid ambiguous, loaded, or difficult words; technical terms; negative constructions; and double-barreled questions.

    - Avoid items that are likely to be answered the same way by most people.

    - Include items that concern both positive and negative aspects of the target.

12. Strive for an attractive and professional design for the questionnaire; this typically involves:

    - a booklet format,

    - economical use of space with full but not overcrowded pages,

    - an orderly layout that utilizes various typefaces and highlighting options, and appropriate sequence marking (of sections and items),

    - good paper quality.

13. In the initial (general) instructions cover the following points:

    - the topic and importance of the study,

    - the sponsoring organization,

- point out that there are no right or wrong answers and request honest responses,

- promise confidentiality,

- thank the participants.

14. In the specific instructions to the tasks exemplify (rather than merely explain) how to answer the questions.

15. Thank the participants again at the end of the questionnaire.

16. Always pilot your questionnaire in a systematic manner and submit the items to item analysis (cf. Section 2.9).

ADMINISTERING THE QUESTIONNAIRE

17. Make the participant sample as representative of the total population you are investigating as possible (cf. Section 3.1.1).

18. Make the sample size large enough to allow for statistically significant results (cf. Section 3.1.2).

19. Beware of participant self-selection (cf. Section 3.1.3).

20. With postal administration:

- Formulate the cover letter very carefully (for a list of points to be covered, see Section 3.2.1).

- Print the return address on the questionnaire as well.

- About 2½ weeks after the original mailing send a follow-up letter, and in another 10 days' time send another one.

- Apply various strategies to increase the return rate (for a list, see Section 3.2.1).

21. With one-to-one administration, make sure that you brief the questionnaire administrator well and consider giving him/her a cue card with the main points to cover when handing out the questionnaires.

22. To increase the quality and quantity of questionnaire response, apply the following strategies:

- Provide advance notice.

- Win the support of the various authority figures.

- Try to arrange some respectable institutional sponsorship for your survey.

- The administrator's overall conduct should be friendly and professional, and he/she should exhibit keen involvement and an obvious interest in the project.

- 'Sell' the survey by communicating well its purpose and significance.

- Emphasize confidentiality.

- Promise feedback on the results for those who are interested (and then remember to provide it…).

23. Observe the various ethical principles and regulations very closely (cf. Section 3.4.1) and obtain the required 'human subjects' approval.

PROCESSING QUESTIONNAIRE DATA

24. As soon as you have received the completed questionnaires, mark each with a unique identification code.

25. Record every important step you take during the processing of the data in a 'Research Logbook.'

26. Prepare a coding frame for each item and record these in a codebook.

27. Always prepare a backup of the data files. Do it now!

28. Submit your data to 'data cleaning procedures' before starting the analyses (cf. Section 4.3.1).

29. Consider the way you handle missing data very carefully.

30. Reverse the scoring of negatively worded items before starting the analyses (cf. Section 4.3.2).

31. Consider standardizing the data before starting the analyses (cf. Section 4.3.2).

32. Start the analyses of your questionnaire data by reducing the number of variables through computing multi-item scales.

33. Compute internal consistency reliability coefficients (Cronbach Alphas) for each multi-item scale.

34. Numerical questionnaire data are typically processed by means of statistical procedures; for most purposes you will need inferential statistics accompanied by indices of statistical significance (cf. Section 4.3.6).

35. Process open-ended questions by means of some systematic content analysis.

36. Exercise great caution when generalizing your results.

37. Make sure that you include all the necessary technical information about your survey in your research report (for a checklist, see Section 4.6.2).

38. Make use of charts/diagrams, schematic representations, and tables as much as possible when reporting your results.

39. Consider complementing your questionnaire data with information coming from other sources.

References

Aiken, L. (1996). Rating scales and checklists: Evaluating behavior, personality, and attitudes. New York: John Wiley.

Aiken, L. (1997). Questionnaires and inventories: Surveying opinions and assessing personality. New York: John Wiley.

Anderson, L. W. (1985). Attitudes and their measurement. In T. Husén & T. N. Postlethwaite (Eds.), *The international encyclopedia of education* (Vol. 1, pp. 352-58). Oxford: Pergamon.

Bardovi-Harlig, K. (1999). Researching method. In L. F. Bouton (Ed.), *Pragmatics and Language Learning* (Vol. 8, pp. 237-264). Urbana-Champaign, IL: University of Illinois, Division of English as an International Language.

Brown, H. D. (1994). *Teaching by principles: An interactive approach to language pedagogy.* Englewood Cliffs, NJ: Prentice Hall Regents.

Brown, H. D. (2000). *Principles of language learning and teaching* (4th ed.). New York: Longman.

Brown, H. D. (2002). *Strategies for success: A practical guide to learning English.* New York: Longman.

Brown, J. D. (2001). *Using surveys in language programs.* Cambridge, UK: Cambridge University Press.

Burstall, C., Jamieson, M., Cohen, S., & Hargreaves, M. (1974). *Primary French in the balance.* Windsor: NFER.

Chamot, A. U., Barnhardt, S., El-Dinary, P. B., & Robbins, J. (1999). *The learning strategies handbook.* New York: Longman.

Clemans, W. V. (1971). Test administration. In R. L. Thorndike (Ed.), *Educational measurement* (2nd ed. pp. 188-201). Washington, DC: American Council on Education.

Clément, R. (1986). Second language proficiency and acculturation: An investigation of the effects of language status and individual characteristics. *Journal of Language and Social Psychology, 5,* 271-290.

Clément, R., & Baker, S. C. (2001). *Measuring social aspects of L2 acquisition and use : Scale characteristics and administration.* Technical Report. Ottawa: School of Psychology, University of Ottawa.

Clément, R., & Kruidenier, B. G. (1983). Orientations on second language acquisition: 1. The effects of ethnicity, milieu and their target language on their emergence. *Language Learning, 33,* 273-291.

Clément, R., & Kruidenier, B. G. (1985). Aptitude, attitude and motivation in second language proficiency: A test of Clément's model. *Journal of Language and Social Psychology, 4,* 21-37.

Clément, R., & Noels, K. A. (1992). Towards a situated approach to ethnolinguistic identity : The effects of status on individuals and groups. *Journal of Language and Social Psychology, 11,* 203-232.

Clément, R., & Dörnyei, Z., & Noels, K. A. (1994). Motivation, self-confidence and group cohesion in the foreign language classroom. *Language Learning, 44,* 417-448.

Cochran, W. G. (1977). *Sampling techniques* (3rd ed.). New York: Wiley.

Cohen, A. D. (1987). Students processing feedback on their compositions. In A. Wenden & J. Rubin (Eds.), *Learner strategies in language learning* (pp. 57-69). Hemel Hempstead, UK: Prentice-Hall.

Cohen, A. D. (1991). Feedback on writing: The use of verbal report. *Studies in Second Language Acquisition, 13,* 133-159.

Cohen, A. D., & Chi, J. C. (2001). *Language Strategy Use Survey.* http://carla.acad.umn.edu/profiles/Cohen-profile.html.

Cohen, A. D., & Dörnyei, Z. (2001).*Taking my Motivational Temperature on a Lnguage Task.* http://carla.acad.umn.edu/profiles/Cohen-profile.html.

Cohen, A. D., & Oxford, R. L. (2001a). *Young Learners' Language Strategy Use Survey.* http://carla.acad.umn.edu/profiles/Cohen-profile.html.

Cohen, A. D., & Oxford, R. L. (2001b). *Learning Styles Survey for Young Learners.* http://carla.acad.umn.edu/profiles/Cohen-profile.html.

Cohen, A. D., Oxford, R. L., & Chi, J. C. (2001). *Learning Style Survey.* http://carla.acad.umn.edu/profiles/Cohen-profile.html.

Coleman, J. A. (1996). *Studying languages: A survey of British and European students.* London: CILT.

Converse, J. M., & Presser, S. (1986). *Survey questions: Handcrafting the standardized questionnaire.* Newbury Park, CA: Sage.

Creswell, J. W. (1994). *Research design: Qualitative and quantitative approaches.* Thousand Oaks, CA: Sage.

Cumming, A. (1991). *Identification of current needs and issues related to the delivery of adult ESL instruction in British Columbia.* Richmond, B. C.: Open Learning Agency. ERIC ED 353 855.

Davidson, F. (1996). *Principles of statistical data handling.* Thousand Oaks, CA: Sage.

Dörnyei, Z. (1990). Conceptualizing motivation in foreign language learning. *Language Learning, 40,* 46-78.

Dörnyei, Z. (2001). *Teaching and researching motivation.* Harlow, UK: Longman.

Dörnyei, Z., & Clément, R. (2001). Motivational characteristics of learning different target languages: Results of a nationwide survey. In Z. Dörnyei & R. Schmidt (Eds.), *Motivation and second language acquisition* (pp. 399-432). Honolulu, HI: University of Hawaii, Second Language Teaching & Curriculum Center.

Dörnyei, Z., & Csizér, K. (in press). Some dynamics of language attitudes and motivation: Results of a longitudinal nationwide survey. *Applied Linguistics.*

Ehrman, M. E. (1996a). *Understanding second language learning difficulties.* Thousand Oaks, CA: Sage.

Ehrman, M. E. (1996b). An exploration of adult language learning motivation, self-efficacy and anxiety. In R. L. Oxford (Ed.), *Language learning motivation: Pathways to the new century* (pp. 103-131). Honolulu, HI: University of Hawaii Press.

Ehrman, M. E., & Dörnyei, Z. (1998). *Interpersonal dynamics in second language education: The visible and invisible classroom.* Thousand Oaks, CA: Sage.

Eignor, D., Taylor, C., Kirsch, I., & Jamieson, J. (1998). *Development of a scale for assessing the level of computer familiarity of TOEFL examinees.* TOEFL Research Report No. 60. Princeton, NJ: Educational Testing Service.

Ellard, J. H., & Rogers, T. B. (1993). Teaching questionnaire construction effectively: The Ten Commandments of question writing. *Contemporary Social Psychology, 17,* 17-20.

Ely, C. M. (1986a). Language learning motivation: A descriptive causal analysis. *Modern Language Journal, 70,* 28-35.

Ely, C. M. (1986b). An analysis of discomfort, risktaking, sociability, and motivation in the L2 classroom. *Language Learning, 36,* 1-25.

Ely, C. M. (1989). Tolerance of ambiguity and use of second language strategies. *Foreign Language Annals, 22,* 437-445.

Fink, A. (1995). *How to report on surveys (The Survey Kit 9).* Thousand Oaks, CA: Sage.

Gardner, R. C. (1985). *Social psychology and second language learning: The role of attitudes and motivation.* London: Edward Arnold.

Gardner, R. C., & Smythe, P. C. (1981). On the development of the Attitude/Motivation test Battery. *Canadian Modern Language Review, 37,* 510-25.

Gardner, R. C., Tremblay, P. F., & Masgoret, A-M. (1997). Toward a full model of second language learning: An empirical investigation. *Modern Language Journal, 81,* 344-362.

Gass, S. M., & Mackey, A. (2000). *Stimulated recall methodology in second language research.* Mahwah, NJ: Lawrence Erlbaum Associates, Inc.

Gillham, B. (2000). *Developing a questionnaire.* London: Continuum.

Gliksman, L., Gardner, R. C., & Smythe, P. C. (1982). The role of the integrative motive on students' participation in the French classroom. *Canadian Modern Language Review, 38,* 625-647.

Green, C. F. (1999). Categorizing motivational drives in second language acquisition. *Language, Culture and Curriculum, 12,* 265-279.

Hart, D., & Cumming, A. (1997). A follow-up study of people in Ontario completing level 3 of the Language Instruction for Newcomers to Canada (LINC) program. Toronto: Ontario Institute for Studies in Education of the University of Toronto. ERIC ED 409 745.

Hatch, E., & Lazaraton, A. (1991). *The research manual.* New York: Newbury House.

Hopkins, K. D., Stanley, J. C., & Hopkins, B. R. (1990). *Educational and psychological measurement and evaluation* (7th ed.). Englewood Cliffs, NJ: Prentice Hall.

Horwitz, E. K. (1985). Using student beliefs about language learning and teaching in the foreign language methods course. *Foreign Language Annals, 18,* 333-340.

Horwitz, E. K. (1988). The beliefs about language learning of beginning university foreign language students. *Modern Language Journal, 72,* 283-294.

Horwitz, E. K. (1996). Even teachers get the blues: Recognizing and alleviating non-native teachers' feelings of foreign language anxiety. *Foreign Language Annals, 29,* 365-372.

Horwitz, E. K., Horwitz, M. B., & Cope, J. (1986) Foreign language classroom anxiety. *Modern Language Journal, 70,* 125-132.

Johnston, B., Kasper, G., & Ross, S. (1998). Effect of rejoinders in production questionnaires. *Applied Linguistics, 19,* 157-182.

Jolliffe, F. R. (1986). *Survey design and analysis.* Chichester: Ellis Horwood.

Kasper, G. (1998). Analyzing verbal protocols. *TESOL Quarterly, 32,* 358-362.

Kassabgy, O., Boraie, D., & Schmidt, R. (2001). Values, rewards, and job satisfaction in ESL/EFL. In Z. Dörnyei & R. Schmidt (Eds.), *Motivation and second language acquisition* (pp. 213-237). Honolulu, HI: University of Hawaii, Second Language Teaching & Curriculum Center.

Kearney, K. A., Hopkins, R. H., Mauss, A. L., & Weisheit, R. A. (1984). Self-generated identification codes for anonymous collection of longitudinal questionnaire data. *Public Opinion Quarterly, 48,* 370-378.

Kondo-Brown, K. (2001). Bilingual heritage students' language contact and motivation. In Z. Dörnyei & R. Schmidt (Eds.) *Motivation and second language acquisition* (pp. 433-459). Honolulu, HI: University of Hawaii, Second Language Teaching & Curriculum Center.

Kormos, J. (1998). Verbal reports in L2 speech production research. *TESOL Quarterly, 32,* 353-358.

Labrie, N., & Clément, R. (1986). Ethnolinguistic vitality, self-confidence and second language proficiency: An investigation. *Journal of Multilingual and Multicultural Development, 7,* 269-282.

Levy, P. S., & Lemeshow, S. (1999). *Sampling of populations: Methods and applications* (3rd ed.). New York: John Wiley & Sons.

Lightbown, P. M., & Spada, N. (1999). *How languages are learned* (Revised Edition). Oxford: Oxford University Press.

Low, G. (1999). What respondents do with questionnaires: Accounting for incongruity and fluidity. *Applied Linguistics, 20,* 503-533.

Macer, T. (April, 1999). Designing the survey of the future. *Research Magazine, Issue 395* (also: http://www.macer.co.uk/arts/28.html).

MacIntyre, P. D., Clément, R., Baker, S. C., & Conrad, S. (in press). Willingness to communicate, social support and language learning orientations of immersion students. *Studies in Second Language Acquisition.*

MacIntyre, P. D., & Gardner, R. C. (1991). Language anxiety: Its relation to other anxieties and to processing in native and second languages. *Language Learning, 41,* 513-534.

MacIntyre, P. D., & Gardner, R. C. (1994). The subtle effects of language anxiety on cognitive processing in the second language. *Language Learning, 44,* 283-305.

Moser, C. A., & Kalton, G. (1971). *Survey methods in social investigation.* London: Heinemann.

Murphey, T. (1996). Changing language learning beliefs: "Appresiating" mistakes. *Asian Journal of English Language Teaching, 6,* 77-84.

Newell, R. (1993). Questionnaires. In N. Gilbert (Ed.), *Researching social life* (pp. 94-115). London: Sage.

Noels, K. A., Pelletier, L. G., Clément., R., & Vallerand, R. J. (2000). Why are you learning a second language? Motivational orientations and self-determination theory. *Language Learning, 50,* 57-85.

Nunan, D. (1988). *The learner-centred curriculum.* Cambridge: Cambridge University Press.

Nunan, D., & Lamb, C. (1996). The self-directed teacher: managing the learning process. Cambridge: Cambridge University Press.

Nunnally, J. C. (1978). *Psychometric theory.* New York: McGraw-Hill.

Oppenheim, A. N. (1992). *Questionnaire design, interviewing and attitude measurement* (New Edition). London: Pinter.

Oxford, R. L. (1990). *Language learning strategies: What every teacher should know*. Boston, MA: Heinle & Heinle.

Oxford, R. L. (1995). *Style Analysis Survey (SAS): Assessing your own learning and working styles*. In J. M. Reid (Ed.), *Learning styles in the ESL/EFL classroom* (pp. 208-215). Boston, MA: Heinle & Heinle.

Popham, W. J., & Sirotnik, K. A. (1973). *Educational statistics* (2nd ed.). New York: Harper and Row.

Reid, J. M. (1995). *Learning styles in the ESL/EFL classroom*. Boston, MA: Heinle & Heinle.

Richterich, R. (1980). *Identifying the needs of adults learning a foreign language*. Oxford: Pergamon (for the Council of Europe).

Robinson, J. P., & Shaver, P. R., & Wrightsman, L. S. (1991). Criteria for scale selection and evaluation. In J. P. Robinson, P. R. Shaver & L. S. Wrightsman (Eds.), *Measures of personality and social psychological attitudes* (pp. 1-16). San Diego, CA: Academic Press.

Robson, C. (1993). *Real world research: A resource for social scientists and practitioner-researchers*. Oxford: Blackwell.

Sanchez, M. E. (1992). Effects of questionnaire design on the quality of survey data. *Public Opinion Quarterly, 56,* 216-217.

Schmidt, R., Boraie, D., & Kassabgy, O. (1996). Foreign language motivation: Internal structure and external connections. In R. Oxford (Ed.), *Language learning motivation: Pathways to the new century* (pp. 9-70). Honolulu, HI: University of Hawaii Press.

Schmidt, R., & Watanabe, Y. (2001). Motivation, strategy use, and pedagogical preferences in foreign language learning. In Z. Dörnyei & R. Schmidt (Eds.) *Motivation and second language acquisition* (pp. 313-359). Honolulu, HI: University of Hawaii, Second Language Teaching & Curriculum Center.

Shaaban, K. A., & Ghaith, G. (2000). Student motivation to learn English as a foreign language. *Foreign Language Annals, 33,* 632-644.

Skehan, P. (1989). *Individual differences in second-language learning*. London: Edward Arnold.

Sudman, S., & Bradburn, N. M. (1983). *Asking questions*. San Francisco, CA: Jossey-Bass.

Warden, C. A., & Lin, H. J. (2000). Existence of integrative motivation in an Asian EFL setting. *Foreign Language Annals, 33,* 535-547.

Wenden, A. (1991). *Learner strategies for learner autonomy*. Hemel Hempstead, UK: Prentice Hall.

Wilson, N., & McClean, S. (1994). *Questionnaire design*. Newtownabbey, Northern Ireland: University of Ulster.

Young, D. J. (Ed.). (1999). *Affect in foreign language and second language learning*. Boston, MA: McGraw-Hill.

Appendix

SELECTED LIST OF PUBLISHED L2 QUESTIONNAIRES

Please note that the use of the term 'questionnaires' in this book does not include 'tests', 'production questionnaires' (e.g., DCTs) or classroom observation schemes (cf. Section 1.1).

I would like to thank all my friends and colleagues who have helped me to compile this list. I am certain that I have unintentionally omitted several valuable published instruments from the list below. I apologize for this.

ATTITUDES (SEE ALSO 'LANGUAGE LEARNING MOTIVATION')

- Wenden (1991): Attitudes questionnaire for self-access; Principles of a learner-centered approach
- Burstall, Jamieson, Cohen and Hargreaves (1974): Teachers' Attitudes Scale (toward research involving them)

BIOGRAPHIC BACKGROUND

- Ehrman (1996a): Biographic Background Questionnaire

CLASSROOM OBSERVATION

- Brown (1994): Teacher observation form; Self-observation form (for teachers)

COMPUTER FAMILIARITY

- Eignor, Taylor, Kirsch and Jamieson (1998): Computer familiarity of TOEFL examinees

FEEDBACK

- Cohen (1987): Feedback Questionnaire (concerning the teacher's marking of an essay)

144

- Cohen (1991): Teachers' choices in feedback on student written work; Students' reactions to teachers' comments on written work

GROUP COHESIVENESS

- See Clément and Baker (2001) under 'Language learning motivation' (also reprinted in Dörnyei, 2001)

IMMIGRANT SETTLEMENT

- Cumming (1991)
- Hart and Cumming (1997)

LANGUAGE ANXIETY

- Brown (2002)
- See Clément and Baker (2001) under 'Language learning motivation'
- Ely (1986b): Language Class Discomfort
- Gardner (1985): French Class Anxiety
- Horwitz, Horwitz and Cope (1986): Foreign Language Classroom Anxiety Scale (reprinted in Young, 1999)
- MacIntyre and Gardner (1991): The Axometer
- MacIntyre and Gardner (1994): Input, Processing, and Output (IPO) scale
- Young (1999): The appendices of this edited volume contain several anxiety scales by Daly and Miller (Writing Apprehension), Gardner and MacIntyre, Horwitz et al. (see above), McCroskey (PRCA – to measure communication apprehension), and Sarason and Ganzern (Test Anxiety Scale).

LANGUAGE CONTACT (QUALITY AND QUANTITY)

- See Clément and Baker (2001) under 'Language learning motivation'

LANGUAGE COURSE EVALUATION

- Brown (2001): Language testing course; Reading course

- See Clément and Baker (2001) under 'Language learning motivation'
- Gardner (1985)

LANGUAGE LEARNER BELIEFS

- Horwitz (1988): Beliefs About Language Learning Inventory (BALLI) (reprinted in Young, 1999)
- Lighbown and Spada (1999)
- Murphey (1996)
- Wenden (1991): How I Think I Learn Best

LANGUAGE LEARNING MOTIVATION

- Brown (2002)
- Burstall et al. (1974): Pupils' Attitudes towards Learning French
- Clément and Baker (2001) contains the complete, multi-dimensional questionnaires used by Clément and Kruidenier (1985), Labrie and Clément (1986), Clément (1986), Clément and Noels (1992), Clément, Dörnyei and Noels (1994)
- Clément and Kruidenier (1983): Language Learning Orientations
- Cohen and Dörnyei (2001): Taking my Motivational Temperature on a Language Task
- Coleman (1996)
- Dörnyei (1990, 2001)
- Dörnyei and Clément (2001): Language Orientation Questionnaire
- Ehrman (1996a): Motivation and Strategies Questionnaire
- Ehrman (1996b)
- Ely (1986a)
- Gardner (1985): Attitude/Motivation Test Battery (AMTB)
- Gardner, Tremblay and Masgoret (1997): Version of the AMTB used in the study
- Green (1999)
- Noels et al. (2000): Language Learning Orientation Scale – Intrinsic Motivation, Extrinsic Motivation, and Amotivation (LLOS-IEA)

- Schmidt, Boraie and Kassabgy (1996) (also contains an Arabic version)
- Schmidt and Watanabe (2001)
- Shaaban and Ghaith (2000)
- Warden and Lin (2000)

LANGUAGE LEARNING STRATEGIES

- Brown (2002)
- Chamot, Barnhardt, El-Dinary and Robbins (1999)
- Cohen and Chi (2001): Language Strategy Use Survey
- Cohen and Oxford (2001a): Young Learners' Language Strategy Use Survey
- Ehrman (1996a): Motivation and Strategies Questionnaire
- Oxford (1990): Strategy Inventory for Language Learning (SILL)
- Schmidt et al. (1996) (also contains an Arabic version)
- Schmidt and Watanabe (2001)

LANGUAGE LEARNING STYLES

- Brown (1994): Extroversion/Introversion Test; Right/Left Brain Dominance Test
- Brown (2000): Learning Styles Checklist
- Brown (2002)
- Cohen and Oxford (2001b): Learning Styles Survey for Young Learners
- Cohen, Oxford and Chi (2001): Learning Style Survey
- Ely (1989): Tolerance of Ambiguity Scale
- Ely (1986b): Language Class Risktaking; Language Class Sociability
- Oxford (1995): Style Analysis Survey (SAS)
- Reid (1995)

LINGUISTIC SELF-CONFIDENCE

- See Clément and Baker (2001) under 'Language learning motivation'

NEEDS ANALYSIS

- Nunan (1988)
- Nunan and Lamb (1996)
- Richterich (1980)

PREFERENCES FOR INSTRUCTIONAL ACTIVITIES

- Brown (2000)
- Schmidt et al. (1996) (also contains an Arabic version)
- Schmidt and Watanabe (2001)

SELF-EVALUATION

- Brown (2002)
- See Clément and Baker (2001) under 'Language learning motivation'
- Ehrman and Dörnyei (1998): Sarah Thurrell's "Self-Assessment Sheet for a Writing Course"
- Kondo-Brown (2001): Language Survey of Second Generation Japanese Americans
- Nunan and Lamb (1996)
- Wenden (1991): Evaluation Guide for Notetaking; Questionnaire for a Good Language Learner

TEACHER ANXIETY

- Horwitz (1996): Teacher Anxiety Scale

TEACHER BELIEFS

- Horwitz (1985): Teacher Belief Scale

TEACHER EVALUATION

- In Clément and Baker (2001) under 'Language learning motivation' (also reprinted in Dörnyei, 2001)
- Gardner (1985)

TEACHER MOTIVATION

- Kassabgy, Boraie and Schmidt (2001): The Teacher's World Survey

TEACHER SELF-EVALUATION

- Nunan and Lamb (1996)

WILLINGNESS TO COMMUNICATE

- MacIntyre, Clément, Baker and Conrad (in press)

Author Index

Subject Index